D1188110

LEARN ADVANCED SPANISH

GET IN THE FAST LANE OF LEARNING ADVANCED SPANISH & LEARNING SPANISH LIKE CRAZY!

SOSUKE TAKAHASHI

Table of Contents

How To Introduce Yourself In Spanish: Expressions And Exercises

Knowing how to introduce yourself in Spanish is incredibly helpful for both in-person socialization as well as language learning. As in English, personal introduction comments and questions in Spanish are quite similar. Many greetings are found for them, such as "Hi." This lesson will show you how to introduce yourself in Spanish, as well as phrases to introduce to others. We will have some samples for you to practice in an immersive test. Let's get rolling...

Introduction in Spanish: words with recording

Before using some of the presentations in Spanish, we normally say HELLO and then add a phrase like Nice or ask the other person, HOW ARE YOU? Two notable examples:

1. Hello! Nice to meet you!

2. Hello! How are you?

The words CÓMO (how) and CUÁL (which) are essential to ask names in Spanish with the questions: How are you called? And what is your name? In general, the personal pronoun YOU is more informal than YOU, but it is also more common. Omitting the personal pronoun in a sentence is normal, but be sure to use the correct verb conjugation for the subject, even if you omit it. Here's a list of ways to introduce yourself in Spanish and ask someone else's name:

Hello! My name is Alex (literal translation)

Hello! My name is Alex.

Hello! (I) My name is Jon (I CALL the conjugation of the verb CALL)

Hello! My name is Jon.

Hello! (I) am Jon. (SOY is known as a form of the verb SER - to be)

Hello! I am Jon

What is your name? (TU is a possessive adjective that refers to EL or ELLA)

What's your name?

What is your name? (SU is a possessive adjective for something that belongs to YOU)

What's your name?

What is your name)? (A bit informal way of asking names)

What's your name?

What is your name)? (A bit formal way in Latin America to ask names)

What's your name?

and you? (How to return a question in Spanish)

Y Tu?

Let's briefly analyze the structure of the presentations in Spanish that we have seen so far. First, the word "TU" in YOUR NAME and "su" in YOUR NAME are possessive adjectives or determiners, while TE and SE are reflexive pronouns. Notice that the verb LLAMARSE (to be called) changes its form depending on the pronoun we use. Grammar is important, but for now, focus on the meaning and pronunciation of the expressions. In other lessons, we will go deeper into different topics of grammar in Spanish.

Expressions to present to other people in Spanish

To introduce someone else in Spanish, we will need the irregular verb SER, which will be used as "ES." For the pronoun "ÉL," it will be used like this: "ÉL

ES..." (He is) and "ERES" for "TÚ" for example: "TÚ ERES..." (You are).

When referring to several people, we will use "SON" in this case, "ELLOS SON..." (They are). When introducing someone else in Spanish, it is important to mention if this person is your friend, family member, or someone else, and for this, you can use possessive adjectives, e.g., ex. "He is my friend" (he is my friend).

Remember that you must use a pronoun that corresponds in gender (masculine/feminine) and number (singular/plural) with the person who is presenting. Here are some examples of presentations in Spanish that you can read and listen to. Pay attention to the pronunciation and try to figure out the grammar rules.

Presentations in Spanish - Introducing other people

Her name is Ana (Introducing a woman - SU is a possessive adjective that means HER)

Her name is Ana

She is Mary (ES is a way of BEING, to be)

She is Mary

What is your name? ("Su" = his)

What's her name?

What are their names? ("Sus" = their)

What are their names?

What's her name)? (How to ask for a third person)

What's her name?

What are their names? (How to ask for third parties)

What are their names?

Let me introduce you to my friend.

Let me introduce my friend to you.

I present to you the new teacher.

I introduce the new teacher to you.

How To Use Greetings And Farewells In Spanish

Greetings and goodbyes in Spanish are part of the essential vocabulary in daily conversations. Being able to use the correct greeting before entering a conversation is a good sign of courtesy, especially when you are speaking to someone for the first time. In this lesson, we will talk about how and when to use Spanish greetings to start a conversation in the language and the goodbye phrases that best fit specific situations. This lesson includes many examples, a video, and interactive quizzes. Let's get started...

The first thing to know about greetings in Spanish is that we use two exclamation points, one at the beginning also one at the end of the sentence or expression, for example. Sayings like "Good morning!" For others, 'Hello!' can be used at any time of day. The list of simple greetings in Spanish, and some words on this subject, are below.

See these samples

First, we have to greet the guests.

First, we have to greet the guests.

Hello! Are you busy?

Hello! Are you busy?

Good morning Mr. Torrez! Sit down, please.

Good morning Mr. Torrez. Please sit down.

Good afternoon Ms. González! Sorry, I'm late.

Good afternoon Mrs. Gonzalez! I am sorry I am late.

Good night! We are glad to see you.

Good evening/night! We are glad to see you.

Ways to answer the question like How are you?

There are different ways of asking "How are you?" in Spanish. "How are you?" it is perhaps the easiest to remember. If you want to sound a little more formal, you can use How are you? and also how has it been? The answer may vary from one country to another, but using the expression "Well, and you?" is acceptable anywhere. Listen to the different ways of saying and responding to "How are you" in Spanish:

How are you)? - (I) am fine, and you?

How are you? - I am fine, and you?

Hi Xander. How have you been? - I feel fine, thank you

Hi Ken. How are you doing? - I am doing well, thanks

How are things, Carlos?

How are things going, Carlos?

More ways to say hello in Spanish

When you meet a new person, you can use the equivalent expression for "Nice to meet you" in Spanish, that is, Mucho gusto! o Nice to meet you! (CONOCER is the translation of "to know" into Spanish). If you already know the person, simply change MEET YOURSELF to SEE YOU, for example, Nice to see you! (Nice to see you!). In both sentences, the preposition EN is optional. Listen to some examples using Nice to meet you! and other similar ways of greeting in Spanish.

Nice to meet Roberto!

Nice to meet you, Roberto!

Nice to meet you!

It is a pleasure to meet you!

How nice to see you, Sandra! - Nice to see you too!

Nice to see you, Sandra! - Nice to see you too

Good to see you.

It is good to see you.

What happened? / What's up? / What do you notice? - This questions varies from a country to another.

What´s up?

To respond to greetings in Spanish, we often repeat the same expressions and add the word TAMBIÉN (also) at the end or before the greeting, for example:

Alice: Nice to meet you! / It's a pleasure!

Juan: Nice to meet you too! / Also, a pleasure!

Farewells in Spanish: examples and pronunciation

Saying goodbye in Spanish

There are many expressions related to goodbyes in Spanish. Using one expression or another depends on the formality of the conversation and many other factors. Farewells in Spanish, like greetings, also need two exclamation points. So much goodbye! Like, See ya! they are very common ways of saying goodbye in Spanish. See you! is a way of saying, "See you!" You can add a time complement such as SOON (soon), TOMORROW (tomorrow), THEN (later), IN A MOMENT (in a moment) after SEE YOU as a way to clarify when you will see the other person. Pay attention to these examples:

Goodbye Roger! See you tomorrow at school

Goodbye Roger! See you tomorrow at school.

Goodbye Ariana! See you!

Goodbye Ariana! See you!

It's time to go. Goodbye!

It is time to go. Bye!

Well, see you soon! I had a great time!

Well, see you soon! I had a good time here.

See you soon then! Please take care!

See you soon then! Please take care!

Saying "See you soon" in Spanish

You may have noticed that the word SEE is used in various expressions. This word comes from the verb VER (to see) and is normally used in farewells in Spanish. In the expression See you! We can replace NOS with TE when we refer to one person, or replace NOS with LOS when referring to several people, for example: See you soon! And see you soon!

Next time you say "See you soon," add "See you later!" To remember this expression, you don't need any pronouns or verbs up to and including the time. See you then! Goodbye! See you tomorrow! However, if you can remember, Bye!, see you! and See you soon!, then you will be able to say goodbye in Spanish in most cases.

Sorry, I have something to do. See you later!

Sorry, I have something to do. See you later!

See you later! Good luck!

See you later! May you do well!

Excuse me; I have to go now. It was good to see it.

Excuse me; I must go now. It was good to see you.

Have a good night! / Have a good night!

Have a good evening/night!

Listening Exercise: Greeting and saying goodbye in Spanish

Listen to a basic conversation using the greetings and goodbyes in Spanish that we covered in the lesson. Listen to the recording and then make notes of the most important details so that you can solve the interactive quiz about it.

Prepositions Of Place In Spanish: Sentences And Exercises

Prepositions like "Sobre" (on) and "Debajo" (under) that are used to denote location are adverbs like "Sobre" (over) and "Underneath" (underneath). We will hear about Spanish prepositions of location in this class. Additional, you will also be able to learn this subject by taking an immersive exam. Let's begin...

Prepositions of location in Spanish

Prepositions are important and widely used in the language. It's a common usage to tell where items are placed, as in: "The desk is in front of the board. It is also possible to use prepositions of place to communicate about the location of places, as in "The bank is next to the hospital." "NEXT TO" is a preposition in all of these sentences.

Sometimes these words could be used without adding a reference object, e.g., ex. "It's on top," but the best way is to use them together with the preposition "DE" together with another object, for example: "It's on top of the box." The following image shows some objects and a list of prepositions of place in Spanish that we could use to indicate the location of an object, for example: "The little penguin is next to the big penguin. " The words in green are prepositions of place.

Asking Where is...? In Spanish

First, to ask about the location of something or someone in Spanish, we need the irregular verb ESTAR. This verb will be used in its ESTÁ form for a single object, as in "Where is the car?" And it will be used as THEY'RE to ask about various things, as in" Where are the cars?" Note that you must use the correct definite article before the noun, which in this case is CARRO. Basically, the questions about the location of things in Spanish will follow the structure:

Where + is / are + item + object (s)?

Listen to two examples below using this structure:

Where is the book? - The book is in the box.

Where is the book? - The book is inside the box

Where are the books? - The books are inside the box

Donde Estan los libros? - The books are inside the box

Forming sentences with ESTAR and prepositions of place in Spanish

ESTAR plays a key role in making sentences with prepositions of place in Spanish. For this, it is also necessary to use the definite articles EL, LA, LOS, LAS, and the indefinite articles UN and UNA before the name of the things, for example, EL HOSPITAL (the hospital) and UNA CAJA (a box). You can use ESTAR with prepositions of place following this structure:

Article + object + being + preposition of place + article + object

"The rule is inside the box" / "The cat is in the vase."

As mentioned above, some prepositions of place in Spanish are represented by two or three words, for example, ENCIMA + DE (over) and EN + MEDIO + DE (between). If we omit a part of the sentence, we could change the meaning of what we want to say. Interestingly, the word DE will change to DEL when used before a masculine noun as HOTEL. Therefore, we must say "from the hotel," not "from the hotel," merging DE with EL to create the word DEL. The same rule applies to the propositions "A + EL," for example: "Next to the dog." Note that some prepositions are interchangeable and could mean the same thing depending on the context, such as "FRONT OF" and "FRONT OF." Pay attention to this group of sample sentences using the prepositions of place in Spanish. Use the player to listen to the examples.

EN- The books are in the basket

The books are in the basket.

INSIDE - The cat is inside the house

The cat is inside the house.

NEXT TO - The books are next to the computer

The books are next to the computer.

OVER / ON TOP OF - The book is on/on the box

The book is in the box.

UNDER - The toy is under the chair

The toy is under the chair.

OUT OF / OUT OF - Cards are out of the trash.

The letters are outside the trash can.

IN FRONT OF / IN FRONT OF - The restaurant is in front of/in front of the hotel.

There is a restaurant in front of the hotel.

BEHIND - She's behind the tall boy

She is behind the tall guy.

ABOVE - The painting is on top of the bookcase

The painting is over the bookcase.

Passage Reading

From English To Spanish

How to learn a language from scratch

Learning a language from scratch in a self-taught way is one of the biggest challenges for languages, especially if you don't have experience.

Aprender un idioma desde cero de forma autodidacta es uno de los mayores desafíos para los idiomas, especialmente si no tienes experiencia.

On this page, I present some ideas that can help you so that the attempts you make are not in vain. They are just starting points for you to experiment, as there is no one foolproof method for everyone.

En esta página, presento algunas ideas que pueden ayudarte para que los intentos que hagas no sean en vano. Son solo puntos de partida para que experimente, ya que no existe un método infalible para todos.

Some only read and listen to materials in the other language, even if they don't understand anything, and they swear that this makes you acquire the language

(I have never tried, but it sounds like it is not a sustainable method ... correct me if I'm wrong)

Algunos solo leen y escuchan materiales en el otro idioma, aunque no entiendan nada, y juran que esto hace que adquieras el idioma (nunca lo he probado, pero parece que no es un método sostenible ... corrígeme si me equivoco)

I have also seen that they begin to translate the newspaper word for word (maybe a day or two is fine, but I think that I would not want to do it anymore) after a few days.

Or else, they pick up a traveler's phrasebook, memorize a few sentences, and look for someone to talk to from day one. (we have to admit, it sounds too scary).

También he visto que comienzan a traducir el periódico palabra por palabra (tal vez uno o dos días está bien, pero creo que no querría hacerlo más) después de unos días.

O bien, toman el libro de frases de un viajero, memorizan algunas oraciones y buscan a alguien con quien hablar desde el primer día. (tenemos que admitir que suena demasiado aterrador).

1. Don't let go

It happened to me very often that right at the end of the semester; it occurred to me to start learning a language. I don't know if it was to avoid facing a lot of tasks that would be difficult for me to do or why, but as you can imagine, the school was first and the two or three words that I learned after a day or two of studying the language were they forgot me in a few weeks.

1. No lo dejes ir

Me pasaba muy a menudo eso justo al final del semestre; se me ocurrió empezar a aprender un idioma. No sé si fue para evitar enfrentarme a muchas tareas que me serían difíciles de hacer o por qué, pero como puedes imaginar, la escuela fue la primera y las dos o tres palabras que aprendí después de uno o dos días. de estudiar el idioma me olvidaron en unas semanas.

I know that sometimes you cannot know when life will make you abandon the progress you are leading, and that anything can be used as a pretext, but do your best to make this attempt the final one.

Sé que a veces no puedes saber cuándo la vida te hará abandonar el progreso que estás llevando y que cualquier cosa puede servir de pretexto, pero haz todo lo posible para que este intento sea el definitivo.

Note: this doesn't really mean that you must find THE perfect method and that you cannot fail or be wrong, but that you are willing to try again when the language or your life gets difficult. That is, you are not going to leave it the first time.

Nota: esto no significa realmente que deba encontrar EL método perfecto y que no puede fallar o equivocarse, sino que está dispuesto a intentarlo de nuevo cuando el idioma o su vida se pongan difíciles. Es decir, no lo vas a dejar la primera vez.

2. Search and accumulate

Since you know which language you want to learn, look for resources in libraries. Sometimes there are audiovisual courses that you can borrow or books with methods for beginners. You can also go to bookstores, but usually, you end up buying very hard-to-read grammars that you never check.

2. Busca y acumula

Ya que sabe qué idioma desea aprender, busque recursos en las bibliotecas. A veces hay cursos audiovisuales que puedes pedir prestados o libros con métodos para principiantes. También puedes ir a las librerías, pero por lo general terminas comprando gramáticas muy difíciles de leer que nunca revisas.

Ask acquaintances you know who speak the language if they have any material they no longer use when they started with the language.

Pregunte a sus conocidos que hablen el idioma si tienen algún material que ya no usan cuando empezaron con el idioma.

And, most fruitfully, search the Internet:

Create a bookmark or favorites folder in your Internet browser (Chrome, Firefox) that says "Greek," for example. There you will save all the links you find. You will not learn anything; you will only collect resources that will serve you in the future.

Y, lo más fructífero, busque en Internet:

Cree un marcador o una carpeta de favoritos en su navegador de Internet (Chrome, Firefox) que diga "griego", por ejemplo. Allí guardarás todos los enlaces que encuentres. No aprenderás nada; solo recolectará recursos que le servirán en el futuro.

Other useful phrases to look for:

Greek for Spanish Speakers, Greek for Beginners, Basic Greek, Greek Course, Easy Greek,

Save a blog post whose title catches your attention or an article that explains the basics (the alphabet, for example).

You may keep a lot of junk, but that shouldn't matter as much to you at this stage.

Otras frases útiles para buscar:

Griego para hispanohablantes, Griego para principiantes, Griego básico, Curso de griego, Griego fácil,

Guarda una publicación de blog cuyo título te llame la atención o un artículo que explique los conceptos básicos (el alfabeto, por ejemplo).

Puede guardar mucha basura, pero eso no debería importarle tanto en esta etapa.

Then, look for videos on YouTube and subscribe to Greek for Spanish-speaking or Sefelizaprendegriego (invention again). The idea is that they are specialized channels. If you don't have an account and can't subscribe, just save the links in the folder above.

If the idea well appeals to you, you can also search for the same in English or another language you already know.

Luego, busque videos en YouTube y suscríbase a griego para hispanohablantes o Sefelizaprendegriego (invento nuevamente). La idea es que sean canales especializados. Si no tiene una cuenta y no puede suscribirse, simplemente guarde los enlaces en la carpeta de arriba.

Si la idea le atrae, también puede buscar la misma en inglés o en otro idioma que ya conozca.

When you have about 15 or 20 bookmarks, close that folder and start doing something else.

Cuando tenga alrededor de 15 o 20 marcadores, cierre esa carpeta y comience a hacer otra cosa.

3. Make time and space

Think about next week and establish an activity that you can exchange for the study of your new language:

Watching TV from 6 to 7 instead of two hours, and from 5 to 6 studying Greek.

(It doesn't have to be an hour. It could be 10 minutes. Really.)

Or, if you don't have an activity to trade, do your best to find a space for 10 to 30 minutes each day. Or more, if you can or if you are in a hurry to learn the language.

3.Haga tiempo y espacio

Piensa en la próxima semana y establece una actividad que puedas intercambiar por el estudio de tu nuevo idioma:

Ver televisión de 6 a 7 en lugar de dos horas, y de 5 a 6 estudiando griego.

(No tiene que ser una hora. Pueden ser 10 minutos. De verdad).

O, si no tiene una actividad para comerciar, haga todo lo posible por encontrar un espacio de 10 a 30 minutos cada día. O más, si puedes o si tienes prisa por aprender el idioma.

Try to make that space after the same activity every day (after waking up, or after bathing, or as soon as you get home, etc.) so that it is easier to remember.

If you desire to write it down, you will study during this week after dinner in a place where you can see it. The chances of it being a futile attempt are decreased.

Trate de hacer ese espacio después de la misma actividad todos los días (después de despertarse, o después de bañarse, o tan pronto como llegue a casa, etc.) para que sea más fácil de recordar.

Si deseas anotarlo, estudiarás durante esta semana después de la cena en un lugar donde puedas verlo. Se reducen las posibilidades de que sea un intento inútil.

4. Find what you like

In the following days, you may begin to learn some words or some things, but the purpose of this stage is to reduce the list of markers that you obtained in step 2. And keep what you like.

Surely there will be pages that you find boring or videos of very poor quality, but you will also find materials that you like a lot. Those are the ones you should save. Erase the markers you didn't like without fear.

4. Encuentra lo que te gusta

En los días siguientes, es posible que empieces a aprender algunas palabras o algunas cosas, pero el propósito de esta etapa es reducir la lista de marcadores que obtuviste en el paso 2. Y quédate con lo que te gusta.

Seguro que habrá páginas que te resulten aburridas o vídeos de muy mala calidad, pero también encontrarás materiales que te gusten mucho. Esos son los que debes salvar. Borra los marcadores que no te gustaron sin miedo.

For example, on the first day of reviewing materials, you will see the first 5 markers you saved.

The first and second were very brief (you erase them after seeing them), and the third catches your attention. It was a video, and that takes you to another and then another. You discover that you like it, and suddenly, the time you were going to dedicate to your language today is over, and you only checked three of the markers. It's fine. The idea of having several is not that you use them all but that you know that you have options.

Por ejemplo, el primer día de revisión de materiales, verá los primeros 5 marcadores que guardó.

El primero y el segundo fueron muy breves (los borras después de verlos), y el tercero te llama la atención. Era un video, y eso te lleva a otro y luego a otro. Descubres que te gusta, y de repente, se acabó el tiempo que ibas a dedicar hoy a tu idioma, y solo marcaste tres de los marcadores. Está bien. La idea de tener varios no es que los uses todos sino que sepas que tienes opciones.

5. Follow what you like

Suppose you loved a video on a YouTube channel that has 74 videos dedicated only to learning Greek. What follows is to get to see them, that is, to use the materials that you liked and that you think may be of more use to you.

Just let yourself be carried away by what makes you learn pleasantly.

It is about finding two or three help materials (blogs, pages, videos, etc.) that can complement each other so that you gradually acquire the language.

5. Sigue lo que te gusta

Suponga que le encantó un video en un canal de YouTube que tiene 74 videos dedicados solo a aprender griego. Lo que sigue es llegar a verlos, es decir, utilizar los materiales que te gustaron y que crees que pueden ser de más utilidad para ti.

Solo déjate llevar por aquello que te haga aprender gratamente.

Se trata de encontrar dos o tres materiales de ayuda (blogs, páginas, videos, etc.) que se puedan complementar para que poco a poco vayas adquiriendo el idioma.

Effective Steps To Learn A Language Quickly

Learn Spanish Quickly

How to learn Spanish effectively? How to master the language of Cervantes and be able to speak Spanish fluently?

Learn the exceptions of a grammar rule, conjugation and irregular verbs, practice the pronunciation of consonants and vowels, intonations, concordances, accents... The list is very long.

Spanish may not be as difficult to learn as Chinese or Arabic, but there are also many difficulties in assimilating all its subtleties and becoming bilingual.

Are you motivated?

Are you already learning Spanish as a foreign language with group classes?

Do you have notions and need to catch up?

Speaking Spanish thanks to movies and cinema

Forget about your Spanish lessons and exercises for a moment and relax a little while working your oral comprehension in front of a good Spanish movie in its original version.

Studying Spanish through cinema can be done regardless of your language level.

If you have a beginner level (A1 or A2), obviously you will have to put the subtitles, but little by little, as you go up to the intermediate level (B1 or B2) and then to the advanced level (C1 or C2), you will be able to watch the movies without having to put them on or stop a scene because you did not understand it, and you will simply enjoy the movie.

At first, you will have to make great efforts to learn not to watch the subtitles too much, but you will see that it is a very instructive exercise, essential for a good learning of the language.

•   Watching Spanish movies to learn to speak the language fluently is a very beneficial learning method in more method than one, as you will be able to learn to:

•   Familiarize yourself with the sounds of the Spanish language (pronunciation, phonetics, intonation, accent...).

•   Enrich your vocabulary: you quickly learn new words when they are placed in context, as is the case in a movie. You will also discover many idiomatic expressions.

•   Discover Spanish culture through the seventh art: language and culture go hand in hand, so by watching Spanish films, you will improve your general culture about Spain, its history, its traditions and its lifestyle.

•   Discovering the spoken language: while the Spanish learning books show a formal language, in the movies, you will be able to discover the different registers of the language.

For this technique to be effective, think that the key is repetition. Schedule a movie session several times a week to make rapid progress in Spanish. And take notes to learn certain words or phrases after watching the movie.

Take a look at the most valued Spanish films and learn Spanish thanks to the cinema!

Learn to speak Spanish with a private teacher

Another tip to progress faster in Spanish: take classes with a teacher. It is the most effective way to learn to communicate in Spanish for several reasons.

First, you benefit from individual teaching and personalized follow-up, adapted to your level and your goals. In general, a private Spanish teacher will start by making a first assessment through a Spanish level test, and will also learn to know you better.

In addition, you will benefit from teaching adapted to your needs, but above all, you will develop a trusting relationship with your teacher, which will allow you to more easily address the notions that are most difficult for you or that is of special interest to you.

If, for example, you plan to go abroad, live in Spain or study Spanish in Madrid, taking private Spanish lessons for foreigners with a native teacher will help you get your questions answered. In this way, you will have a valuable help to prepare for your future life change:

How to integrate in Spain?

What are the cultural habits to know?

What is the Spanish way of life?

How to learn to carry on a conversation in Spanish?

In short, taking private Spanish classes implies progressing faster and more efficiently with respect to a specific objective, such as improving speaking skills. While in a group class you may have difficulties practicing your oral expression, with private classes it is easier to overcome your fears and practice much more.

If you feel that you are no longer making progress in your Spanish learning and you are stuck, turning to a specialized teacher to take individual classes is a guarantee of success to improve your skills and speak Spanish more easily.

Speaking Spanish: how to get it thanks to the applications

When learning Spanish, to improve your language skills effectively, it is important to use all the teaching materials that are available, and taking into account the reality we live in today, it will be more than easy for you to find an ELE course online.

Language learning requires intensive and regular practice, so the best way to practice anywhere and at any time of the day is to download apps to learn Spanish.

Thanks to the applications, you can access Spanish lessons and exercises on your mobile or tablet. At any time of the day, it is very easy to improve your Spanish with interactive exercises, review your Spanish vocabulary, work on your oral expression or learn new rules of Spanish grammar.

To help you learn Spanish, here is a selection of essential applications, for all levels, to achieve a good level in Spanish as a foreign language:

If you want to learn Spanish quickly, in summary:

- Learn while having fun, watching a good movie, for example.
- Vary the teaching materials to improve your Spanish.

- Take a language immersion to become perfectly bilingual.
- Take a course in Spanish language, either with a private teacher, evening classes, intensive courses or language schools.
- You will be surprised on how quickly you progress in learning Spanish!

How To Learn To Speak Spanish Quickly

Admit that if you are reading this section, you only want one thing: learn to speak Spanish quickly!

Unfortunately, Spanish can be difficult to learn as it is a complex language. Many foreign students have said it for years.

Furthermore, even for us Spaniards, Spanish has exceptions and rules that we do not fully control.

Tips to learn Spanish quickly:

Read Spanish newspapers: El Mundo, 20 minutes, El País, ABC...

Learn a little vocabulary every day: make flashcards and repeat them daily,

Learn the conjugation: you must know at least how to perfectly conjugate the present tense at the beginning,

Learn the basic rules of grammar,

Listen to Spanish TV, songs, movies or podcasts to practice your listening skills...

There are many ways to achieve your goal. Set goals to progress gradually!

If you want to take a Spanish teacher course for foreigners, do not hesitate to sign up for our service.

Films To Study The Language Of Cervantes

Taking Spanish classes is essential, but how not to get discouraged when difficulties arise? Just learning while having fun!

Do you love to relax in the cinema or in front of a good movie on your sofa? It is an excellent opportunity to improve your Spanish as a foreign language.

So is watching movies to learn to speak Spanish a good idea? The answer is definitely yes. It is a good option when you cannot learn Spanish in Spain by doing a language exchange, an Erasmus or a Spanish course.

Watching movies in VO is also a good solution if you want to learn Italian, English, German, and Portuguese... In short, to learn any language you want!

Spanish cinema, inseparable from Spanish culture

Invented by the Lumière brothers in 1894, the cinema was a true revolution at that time. Since then, the seventh art has been an integral part of Spanish culture.

Spanish cinema is among the most prolific in the world and enjoys an excellent reputation beyond our borders.

In Spain we have film festivals whose reputation is unsurpassed, such as the San Sebastián Film Festival. These events help reinforce the positive image of Spanish cinema in the world.

It's assumed that it is not necessary to convince and encourage you to watch Spanish films as a complement to your Spanish classes for adult foreigners. It is an exercise that will be very beneficial and will help you improve your Spanish, if you follow some essential recommendations.

Are you also interested in knowing how to learn Spanish quickly?

Good reasons to watch movies on VOSE to speak Spanish

If you watch movies in Spanish to improve your command of the language, you will enjoy the pleasure of learning differently. You can easily progress and develop your vocabulary, but not only that.

Watching Spanish films in their original version implies totally immersing yourself in the language and thus you will be able to:

- Work on your oral comprehension: there is nothing better to learn to understand spoken Spanish than listening to native speakers. Movies have the advantage that they immerse you directly in spoken language. This way you will accustom your ear to the Spanish sounds and you will have less comprehension difficulties.
- Learn new words: vocabulary is one of the keys to being fluent in Spanish. If you have already learned the basic concepts of the Spanish language (grammar, conjugation ...), you just need to expand your vocabulary in Spanish.
- Discover a culture: Spanish films are a reflection of Spanish culture. From popular hits to art cinema and auteur cinema, with each film you will learn a little more about the particularities of Spanish culture and the way of life of the Spanish, as well as the history of the country and the most important personalities. Important of Spain.
- Discover the spoken language of everyday life: as a film is always a reflection of an era and a reality, you will get rid of the typical Spanish clichés and discover the different registers of the language.

How to learn to speak Spanish in front of a movie?

To get the most out of your movie sessions, it is important that you follow some recommendations.

As you know, when learning a language, one of the keys to success is assiduity and regularity. Therefore, it is important, and it is valid at all levels, that:

- You watch movies regularly

- Do not be discouraged,

- Enjoy these film sessions in VO.

To optimize your learning independently, you will have to adapt the way you watch the films according to your level (A1, A2, B1, B2...).

If you have a beginner level:

Choose to watch movies that you have already seen in your native language. It will be less intimidating because you will already know the story.

- Put the subtitles: at the beginning, if you have problems understanding the dialogues in Spanish, they will help you, so you will have simultaneously the translations of the words that you do not know.
- Feel free to pause: while it's not the best way to appreciate a movie, rewatching a scene can be useful when you don't understand dialogue, for example.
- Take notes: this is a great opportunity to enrich your vocabulary, so take the opportunity to jot down some useful expressions.

- Repeat the dialogues: practice, repeating a dialog for example, to better pronounce Spanish. Repeating the phrase while trying to respect intonation and pronunciation is the best way to improve your oral expression.

In this way, you will then advance faster in your Spanish for foreigners.

If you already have a good level of Spanish (intermediate level, advanced level):

- Put on movies you don't know: if necessary, quickly read the summary that explains the plot and characters to help you understand.
- Do not put subtitles or, in any case, in Spanish. It is a good solution to make a movie easier to understand. Instead of having the translation, you can combine written comprehension and oral communication.
- Put back scenes that you find difficult to study them more accurately and take notes.

Mistakes to avoid

For this exercise to be effective and to improve your ELE level, it is important to have good habits. In general, when you start watching Spanish movies, you can make some mistakes, for example:

- Wanting to understand every word: Unless you are already bilingual, there will always be words that you don't understand in a sentence, but this should not block you. Try to understand the meaning of the sentence to deduce the most probable meaning.
- Lack of perseverance: it takes regularity to become familiar with this exercise, so it is recommended that you organize movie sessions on a regular basis. You don't need to do a movie marathon, but watching two or three a week is very effective.
- Focus on the subtitles: If you only watch the subtitles, you will not enjoy the movie - try to watch them as little as possible. If you really haven't understood something, you can always replay the scene to read the subtitles.
- See a movie only once: the key to learning Spanish for foreigners is repetition. Do not hesitate to see a movie that you already know. You will realize that many details will have escaped you the first time.

Selection Of Essential Films To Speak In Spanish

Spanish cinema has such varied films that you can choose according to your tastes from a multitude of works.

Here is a more general collection that can help you explore more recent films and other classic productions, but they are all part of the Spanish cinematic heritage.

- C-211 (2009). On the day Juan Alberto Ammann begins serving as a corrections officer, he gets embroiled in a prison riot. After posing as another inmate, he ends the uprising, instigated by Malamadre (Luis Tosar).
- proposition (1996). Image student Angela is writing a paper on audiovisual crime. Her boss offers to scan the faculty video library for extra videos, but the next day he is found dead.
- others (2001). The war is over, but Nicole Kidman's husband does not return. She educated her children within of strict religious rules on the Isle of Jersey. However, situations outside of Grace's influence will contradict her stringent instructions.
- Pan's Maze (2006). 1944: Postwar Spanish Ivana (Baquero) and her mother, Carmen (Gil), travel to a small town in which Carmen's new husband, Vidal (López), is assigned to the military. One night, Ofelia encounters a faun (Doug Jones), who shares a disturbing truth to her.
- is approaching" (1995). St. John wrote in the Apocalypse that the Antichrist will be born on December 25, 1995 in Madrid.
- The Sea Inside (2004). For almost thirty years, Ramón (Javier Bardem) has been bedridden with his relatives. He has the only view into the

universe for him to be able to see the sea, which interrupts his childhood. He's died attempting to achieve that goal.

- impossible (2012). Maria, Henry, and their three young children travel from Japan to Thailand for the Christmas holidays on the beach. A tremendous tsunami levels a wide portion of Southeast Asia's coastline.
- The culture (2000). There are 300 million dollars hidden in a flat. She goes to the apartment upstairs and hides the money, but must face the deranged neighborhood group who will do its possible to keep her and the fortune.
- Close your eyes (1997). When he inherited his parents' wealth, César built himself a beautiful mansion and held extravagant parties every night. One night, meeting Sofía, Nuria falls in love with him and dies of envy. Driving with César the following day, she commits suicide. Waking up in the hospital, Cesar learns that his face has been badly disfigured.
- the divine infants (1984). Francos España In the 1960s, a poor family lived in an Extremadura farmhouse owned by the landowner. There is no avoiding their plight until the unexpected happens.

A course tailored for foreigners to support them with their Spanish is recommended before coming to Spain to learn Spanish. Watch movies, too.

Educational supports can be enjoyed and/or varied depending on individual choice. Community practices are a safe way to maintain good language learning: language and culture are inseparable.

- It is a wonderful chance to learn Spanish, but it also increases your fluency. Also, you can learn Spanish on your television computer.
- Learning a foreign language in general calls for using various educational tools to speed up progress.
- Your Spanish instructor for foreigners will motivate you, and why not, talk about a particular movie. Spanish is taught better using this form!

Private Classes To Learn The Language Of Cervantes

There are many possibilities to learn the language of Cervantes: Spanish classes for adults, language schools, group classes, Spanish as a second language, intensive courses, evening classes, immersion courses... But in this section, we focus on the classes Spanish individuals.

What are the merits of learning Spanish with private lessons?

How to find the ideal tutor?

Thanks to the Spanish classes you will be able to familiarize yourself with the language, develop your language skills effectively and progress quickly to speak Spanish with complete confidence.

The interest of private classes to learn Spanish

What are the reasons for taking ELE classes for adults with a private teacher? There are some. Among the most obvious, we can mention:

•   Save time: classes at home will save you time, since you will not have to travel. Your teacher will go directly to your home to teach you Spanish as a foreign language.

•   Enjoy personalized classes: it is undoubtedly one of the best reasons to opt for private Spanish classes, since the teacher adapts to the needs of your student and offers personalized follow-up according to their level, the time available, their objectives, but also your tastes and your favorite teaching methods.

•   Improve faster: thanks to personalized tracking, you will progress faster. With group classes, we often don't even listen to the teacher or the other students. However, private classes are an exchange between two people, so the student will speak in Spanish much more frequently. The teacher will also be able to correct errors more effectively and review the concepts that the student needs.

•   Make the investment profitable: the private classes are not free, as you know, but you can make your investment profitable, and when you see how quickly you progress in Spanish with the private classes, you will realize that this type of training is very affordable. Private teachers generally adapt their prices according to various criteria: student level, teacher studies, discounts according to the number of classes, free first class...

•   Limit restrictions: private classes also give you the possibility to learn to communicate in Spanish without altering your entire schedule. If you enroll in a language school, for example, it is the student who must adapt to the class schedule, while with a private teacher; the student can choose the schedule that best suits them according to their availability. You also have the possibility to save time by taking webcam classes, for example, at any time of the day.

Learn The Basics Of Spanish

Thanks to your private Spanish classes for foreigners, you will be able to learn the basics of the language and get the most out of the advice of a bilingual teacher in Spanish or native.

To feel comfortable speaking Spanish, it is important to master the essential aspects of the language such as:

• The Spanish grammar and exceptions,

• The Spanish conjugation (present, past, imperfect, future simple, conditional...),

• The concordance of the times,

• The agreement of gender and number,

• Spelling rules and vocabulary in Spanish,

• Phonetics, intonation and pronunciation,

• Accents, etc.

Written and oral expression, written and oral comprehension are also part of the aspects that must be mastered in a language.

With a private teacher, you can, depending on your level (beginner, intermediate, advanced...), address all these essential notions.

It is convenient to do a first level test so that your teacher detects your strengths and weaknesses so that he can adapt his classes.

If you are a beginner or need to catch up in Spanish, you will be able to acquire the basic concepts of the Spanish language, work on your oral expression, and learn to make correct sentences while respecting the grammatical structure...

The classes allow you to tackle certain notions, learning the rules of Spanish, but also putting it into practice with different exercises, games, conversations...

Your teacher will be able to vary the teaching approaches to help you progress quickly in Spanish, depending on your abilities.

Would you like to know how to learn Spanish through the cinema?

Learn Spanish: How to Choose a Good Teacher

To start with your private ELE classes, you have to find the teacher who meets your expectations. Before starting to search, it is important that you are clear about your objectives and the reasons that lead you to take Spanish classes.

Is it to travel?

For your studies?

To prepare for an exam?

To live in Spain or in a Spanish-speaking country?

Because of work?

Because of your taste for languages?

The reasons that motivate you can be very diverse and will help you determine the content of the classes you need. When one learns a language, it is to be able to speak it correctly in a certain context; your priorities will not be the same whether you want to learn Spanish for travel or to use it in a professional environment.

You will also have to determine your level before looking for your private teacher. Do you have no notion of Spanish or, on the contrary, is it a language that you have already begun to learn and want to consolidate your knowledge?

So you can know what types of classes are most suitable for you:

- Conversation classes
- Professional Spanish classes,
- Introductory classes,
- Advanced classes,
- Classes to catch up,
- Exam preparation classes,
- Classes for adults,
- Classes for children,

Once you gotten a clearer idea of the type of ELE course that is best for you, you just need to find a private teacher that meets your criteria.

For example, in Superprof, you will be able to find in just a few clicks a teacher of Spanish for foreigners who offers the type of classes you are looking for. Among the search criteria, you can specify your level and choose according to the teachers' profiles and their prices.

There are almost 4400 ELE teachers enrolled in Superprof. Depending on the profile, the prices vary a lot. Do not hesitate to have a look at the teachers present in your city!

Learning Spanish: How Do You Develop A Private Lesson?

The first private lesson in a language is intended to introduce yourself, get to know yourself better and determine the student's objectives, but it is also the perfect opportunity to carry out an initial assessment of the student's level to plan the content of the classes.

Your Spanish teacher will make sure to offer you classes that meet your needs and goals.

If you want to learn Spanish for foreigners in order to travel around the world and discover different cultures, classes can, for example, be more focused on oral expression and comprehension to be able to communicate more easily in specific situations (ask in a restaurant, ask for directions, book a hotel...). It will also be an excellent opportunity to unite language with culture.

If you already have a good level in Spanish but want to learn to speak the language fluently in a professional environment, you can take weekly classes focused on this area of Spanish (specific vocabulary, most used expressions, etc.).

In any case, whatever the content of your Spanish classes, they are generally carried out in several stages:

- Go back to the previous lesson and correction of the possible exercises,
- Lesson of the day, around a specific topic (grammar, conjugation, spelling, reading, conversation ...) based on a supporting document, whether visual, written or audio,
- Exercises to put into practice the lesson addressed,
- Personal work for the next class (online exercises, lessons to learn, vocabulary to review...).

Language learning requires regular and assiduous work, so to improve your Spanish, feel free to practice the language daily, between classes. Your private teacher can also give you good advice and provide you with educational resources to complete your classes and help you study Spanish independently to progress more easily:

- Websites dedicated to learning Spanish,
- Applications to learn Spanish,
- Online Videos...

This is one of the advantages of private classes at home: you develop a relationship of trust with your teacher whose objective is to help you in your learning of Spanish as a foreign language, while developing your taste for learning.

Our teachers will be able to teach you to read and pronounce Spanish, to discover Spanish culture, to improve your oral expression and to master all the subtleties (not to mention difficulties) of Spanish.

After a few months, you will have already made significant progress to be able to carry out your projects:

- Language stay,
- Live in Spain,
- University studies abroad,
- Working in a Spanish-speaking country...

Spanish is the second spoken language in the world, so learning it will open up many possibilities: go to Spain to live in Madrid or Seville and be completely bilingual thanks to linguistic immersion, being one of the many international students that the country welcomes or discover many dream destinations around the world!

Adverbial Phrases Or Expressions To Express Yourself Better Than Anyone Else In Spanish

Convenient Spanish adverbial phrases Sentence adverbials are two or three words that have a particular sense and entity. They change a way of speaking, and respond to an adverb in a phrase.

Example:

From time to time I like to do some exercise you have to try little by little.

They are formed by combining prepositions and nouns, or also adverbs and / or adjectives. Some linguists divide them by classes or types:

- Of time:

- Instantly: The bulls of the Sanfermines left the corral instantly (as soon as the rocket rang).
- Cover to cover: The architects walked the building from cover to cover (from start to finish).
- At night: Mary and Joseph arrived at the Bethlehem portal at night.
- At dusk: At dusk we lit a bonfire on the beach.
- At noon: At noon I left work.

- Of place:

- in between: There were those who got in the way (in the discussion).
- up close: I want to see horses up close.
- in the distance: I saw the guards arrive in the distance.
- high: When you win you will come out with glory high.
- from behind: You were attacked from behind.

- Quantity:

- I miss : I miss you, darling.
- in nothing: In nothing will be September and we will study again.
- Neither more nor less: The guy is the president of the United States.
- I almost didn't survive the crash.

- So:

- blind: I was walking blindly through the dark grotto.
- on foot: He went home on foot.
- by dint of: Only by force of will you will be able to fulfill your dreams.
- left and right: Hit him with the stick left and right (without contemplations)

- Of doubt:

maybe: Maybe take two bags instead of one, just in case.

- Affirmation:

of course: Of course, you cannot go through life insulting people.

- in effect: In effect, Paco is the diminutive of Francisco.
- really: I really just wanted water, but thank you.
- without a doubt: Without a doubt, to pass you have to study.

of course: -Can I go to Jaime's house? - Of course.

- Denial

- in my life: In my life I have been as outdated as the youth of today.
- no longer: No longer content with breaking his bicycle, he threw it in the trash.
- never ever: You will never ever see me napping.

Words In Spanish That Change Your Article

Some words of feminine gender in the Spanish language change the article 'la' for 'el' to avoid sounding bad (cacophony). It occurs when the feminine article 'la' and a feminine noun that begins with a tonic or ha- converge.

For this reason, we do not say 'the water', but we do say 'the water'.

Also, remember that the plural of these words maintains its article corresponding to its gender, 'las'.

That is why we say:

'The waters'.

Here is a list of these 31 words in Spanish that you must learn to know which names change their singular article 'la' for 'el'.

1. the minutes - the minutes - the record - minutes

2. the agate - the agates - the agate - a agate

3. el agua - las aguas - the water - a água

4. the eagle - the eagles - the eagle - a eagle

5. the wing - the wings - the wing - a wing

6. el alga - las algas - the seaweed - a alga

7. the algebra - the algebras - the algebra - a algebra

8. the soul - the souls - the soul - a soul

9. el alza - las alzas - the raise– or increase

10. el ama - las amas - the housewife - a dona

11. el anca - las ancas - the frog's legs - a coxa

12. the anchor - the anchors - the anchor - a âncora

13. the amphora - the amphorae - the amphora - a ânfora

14. the soul - the souls - the soul - a soul

15. the craving - the craving - the longing - a ânsia

16. the ark - the arks - the ark - a ark

17. the area - the areas - the area - a area

18. the weapon - the weapons - the weapon - a weapon

19. the harp - the harps - the harp - a harp

20. the art - the arts - the art - a art

21. el asa - las asas - the handle - a asa

22. the asthma - the asthmas - the asthma - a asthma

23. el aspa - las aspas - the sail - a aspa

24. el asta - las astas - the horn - o chifre

25. el aula - las aulas - the classroom - a aula

26. the aura - the auras - the aura - a aura

27. the bird - the birds - the bird - a ave

28. el haba - las habas - the bean - a fava

29. the speech - you speak - the speech - a fala

30. the ax - the axes - the ax - o stained

31. the fairy - the fairies - the fairy - a fada

Ways To Say "OK" (Yes) In Spanish

"Of course!", "Of course!", "Take it for granted!" They are ways of showing our agreement in Spanish. Here are 30 ways to say OK "yes" in Spanish. "

1.- yes (yes)

2.- ok (all right)

3.- agree (all right)

4.- totally agree

5.- good

5.- very good! (Very good!)

7.- it seems good to me (is very good)

8.- deal done! (Done deal!)

9.- take it for granted! (Consider it done!)

10.- done! (Done!)

11.- oK (ok)

12.- of course! (of course!)

13.-of course it is! (of course!)

14.- indeed (indeed)

15.-why not? (why not?)

16.- of course! (of course!)

17.- of course! (of course!)

18.- aha (aha!)

19.- okay (all rigth)

20.- perfect! (perfect!)

21.- great! (great!)

22.- for you, whatever (for you whatever)

23.- correct (correct)

24.- for you, anything (for you anything)

25.- I can't say no to you (I can't say no to you)

26.- dale / Argentina (all right)

27.- sale / Mexico) (all right)

28.- you win (you win)

29.- do not hesitate! (don't hesitate!)

30.- Without a doubt! (definitely!)

100 Verbs To Start Speaking Spanish

In Practica Español, we have chosen the hundred most necessary verbs to express ourselves in Spanish. Verbs have those functions of indicating the actions we carry out. That is why you cannot speak any language without using them.

However, there are verbs that are more necessary than others to speak; for example," ser" and "estar." Or again, h aber, t ener, say, eating, living, dying...

Each also has several synonyms that add a nuance. Thus, related to "having" we can find "exist", "occur", "be present", etc.; of "having", "possessing"; to "say", "explain", "speak", "add", etc.; to "live" also to "exist", more to "inhabit (a home)", and to die, "perish", "expire", and so on.

Examples:

There was a cat on the roof.

I have three new cards, / I have three new cards.

María told me not to forget about the purchase either / María added not to forget about the purchase.

I live in Madrid / I live in Madrid.

My grandfather died last spring / My grandfather passed away last spring.

The one hundred verbs that we have chosen will help you communicate in the Spanish language, in everyday environments such as work, teaching, routine life, housing, a transfer, a trip, etc.

Some you will use in daily expressions, such as to indicate that you like something or to tell what you have done or what has happened to you.

Examples:

I like pink sauce

I finally managed to send the letter.

They gave me a puppy!

Others are actions in themselves; that is, you can perform them at the same time:

What did you do the other day? (It's a question, so it could be rephrased as "I asked Pablo what he did the other day").

Don't reply to me! (Equivalent to "Ernesto yelled at me / exclaimed not to reply").

The 100 verbs are:

Be   - to be - be

Be - to be -   be

Say - to say - dizer

Come -   to come -   vir

Go -   to go -   go

Speak -   to talk -   falar

Have   - to have -   ter

Do - to do - fazer

haber - there + to be / to have (auxiliary) - haber

Put - to put - place

Duty - must / to have to - dever

Power - can - power

Exit - to exit - sair

Enter - to enter - enter

Write - to write - escrever

Call - to call - chamar

Dance - to dance - dance

Sort - to order   - sort

Visit - to visit   - visit

Travel -   to travel   - travel

Search - to search   - seek

Find - to find -   find

Celebrate - to celebrate   - celebrate

Give away   - to give away   - give away

Fix   -   to fix   -   repair

Work - to work   - trabalhar

Study   - to study   -   study

Form -   to form -   form

Learn - to learn - learn

Create - to create -   raise

Shoot / film -   to shoot / film - film

Investigate   - to investigate -   investigate / research

prepare - to prepare -   prepare

cook - to cook -   cozinhar

Dinner -   to have dinner - jantar

Breakfast - to have breakfast -   drink or café da manhã

Lunch -   to have lunch -   almoçar

Snack -   to have picnic / to have an afternoon snack
- snack

Drink - to drink - drink

Fly - to fly   -   voar

Stroll - to walk   - stroll

Walk - to walk   -   caminhar

March - to march -   march

Run - to run   -   run

See - to watch / to see   -   see

Observe - to observe   -   observe

Look - to look / to see   -   olhar

Use - to use   - use

Communicate - to comunicate - communicate-se

Record -   to record   -   tax

Sleep   - to sleep   - sleep

Awakening - to wake up - wake up

Make - to draw / to take outtake

Sit down - to sit   - sit down

Join - to link   - link

Flirt - to flirt   - seduce

Jump - to jump   - jump

Sing   - to sing   - sing

Prove - to taste / test   -   prove

Like - to like   - gostar

Read - to read   -   ler

Listen   - to listen   -   escutar

Swim - to swim - swim

Clean - to clean   - limpar

Practice -   to practice   - practice

Up -   to get up   - up

Give (turn)   - to turn around   -   give (a volta)

Turn - to turn   -   turn

Dress - to dress up   - dress

Live - to live   - live

To die - to die   - to die

Deliver   - to deliver   - deliver

Send - to send   - send

Attack - to attack   - attack

Hurt - to hurt - ferir

Appease - to appease -   apaziguar

Sign -   to firm   - sign

Get drunk - to get drunk   - intoxicate-se / imebedar-se

Welcome - to welcome -   acolher

Admit - to admit   -   admit

Apply - to apply for r -   apply

Book   - to book - book

Buy   - to buy   - buy

Win   - to win -   ganhar

Share   - to share -   share

Save -   to save -   save

Help -   to help -   ajudar

Save   - to keep/save -   save

Reaffirm   - to reaffirm   -   reaffirm

Assent   - to agree   - assent

Deny   - to deny   - deny

Go up   -   to rise -   go up

Descend - to descend   - baixar / decer

Premiere   - to release   -   premiere

Stain   - to stain   -   stain

Wet   - to wet / dip   -   molhar

Dry -   to dry   -   dry

Play - to play - play

Lodge - to lodge - lodge-se

How many people speak Spanglish and where do they speak it?

Although Spanglish is not the official language of any place, it is a very interesting linguistic phenomenon that is part of the daily life of many Hispanics.

Unfortunately, it happens to me that when I hear the word Spanglish the first thing that comes to mind is a (very mediocre) Adam Sandler movie with the same name. Spanglish is a bilingual language. It can become very interesting to people who have to pick between English and Spanish every day.

What is Spanglish?

As the name implies, Spanglish is a hybrid between Spanish and English, although there is some disagreement about what this actually means. There is no "standard" Spanglish and there are no official rules about how it is spoken. It is the term generally used when someone combines linguistic signs of Spanish and English in their speech. Depending on where it is spoken, it can be more Spanish or more English. One of the easiest examples to recognize is its establishment in music culture since the 90s:

Some linguists argue that Spanglish is only a type of code-switching, or language switching, for example, "I have no money." If this hypothesis were right,

Spanglish will be shallow. Some people claim that Spanglish applies to a more complicated mixture of languages, as a blend of Spanish words would be best classified as a dialect, such as Chicano English.

Pidgin linguists agree that Spanglish is more substantive than a dialect. To connect, two communities without a shared language collide, so they create a new language merging their two native languages. Spanglish is no less nuanced than any other language and is not used to exchange between Hispanics and English speakers. Those who speak Spanglish can even speak Spanish and English fluently.

In Spanglish, another occurrence is word borrowing, or when English words are borrowed and Hispanicized. Several examples are "janguear" (hang out in English), "troca" (truck), "jocho" (hot dog), and "la archive" (from English carpet).

When did you begin speaking Spanish?

People assume Spanglish is a contemporary language. Spanglish has existed since the Treaty of Guadalupe Hidalgo, which formed the present-day U.S.-Mexico frontier, ended. Spanglish's presumed beginnings date back to many years ago, when English tourists visited Spain.

Your speech signifies party affiliation.

Most generally, Spanglish is used in Latino-heavy areas. Cradles in Spanglish apply to these areas. For eg, the language of Cubans is called cubonics.

People will speak Spanglish even though they can speak English, Spanish, or both. Many view Spanglish as a tongue of pride in their Latino culture. Your voice belongs to a faction. For us Latinos, Spanglish is how we act, how we see the world, and how we communicate.

A Spanglish future?

Spanish, in general, is criticized for a decline in American culture. Spanish has been in the US for decades, but this is unlikely. The sky has not collapsed yet. Minority as it combines two languages. Behind the naysayers, Spanglish is here to stay and is being labeled American slang. The 2017 album Despacito integrates Spanish was released in Spanish as "Despacito" in 2016.

People predict that Spanglish would evolve in a similar way to Yiddish, a German-Hebrew hybrid that originated in 13th-century Germany with German Jews. People see the abrasive nonstandard laddish In time, Yiddish became important to many people, and 3 million people speak it today. Many people want to understand this language even though they don't know it.

Spanglish may well have a place in preparing for the future if it is not accepted as an official language.

Olivia, ¡intercultural bilingüe educación!

Being Latino and an immigrant in the United States is difficult for many parents who want their children to assimilate but still preserving their cultural identity.

How to keep Spanish at home.

Before we got pregnant, we determined that we would raise our children bilingual (Spanish and English in our case). The decision is not a whim; however, our first language is Spanish. Olivia was born 5 years ago, with two children, Matías (3 years old) and Lucas (9 months old), who are now homebabies. We've always tried to give our children an intercultural education, thinking that only making them learn their native language is the only way to guarantee their first language is Spanish.

Talk Spanish in the US

To be frank, living in the United States means English is the most important thing, not something else. Legacy problems are among the key factors. While my children are supposed to learn English, I do want them to be bilingual and at least one of their two languages is Spanish, as it is my husband's native language and ties him to his Argentine roots.

As individuals who live in the US and have Latino origins, people in their eagerness to learn English suppress the use of Spanish at home. Thus, kids are cut off from their families' traditions and languages. "You have to know where you came from in order to know where you're going".

It's easier to be bilingual.

For me, language and motherhood are intertwined. Named the mother tongue because it is passed down from women to boy. For me, the scientific truth is just the icing on top of all the research and studies on bilingualism. My presence at "the school in Spanish" on Saturdays in Queens helps me to avoid skipping birthdays, athletic practices, or other extracurricular activities. My inspiration in bilingual parenting comes from my heart, not my brain. My heart needs to be linked to my children. My heart needs to show in my girls.

I deeply agree that making our children taste a sampling of our cuisine, music, traditions, relatives, and the Spanish language unites us as a family. For starters, every week we make empanadas and this involves having tapas in a typical Latin American market with Latin American products. One of our favorite games is "I see, I see," a color-based guessing game that is perfect for road rides or waiting rooms. Any time someone asks us what to bring from Argentina, we order books in Spanish for the girls.

Spanish is yours

"Do you have anything for me today?" Olivia inquires as I return from college. "Here's a new term for you," I tell him. Family photos are shown, along with family members and memories. We address our rituals and celebrations. To instill in you Spanish and US pride, that is my strategy. Language acquisition should be viewed as something to be proud of to our children. At home, Olivia speaks Spanish with me, her dad, and her brothers, but she spends much of her time playing and studying in English.

My children aren't just learning to speak Spanish, but they're also learning to read and write it. They will speak to their grandparents, aunts, uncles, and cousins in their language. When brothers continue to talk entirely in English, the difficulty rises every year. I realize that sometimes I'm exhausted and don't want to work on the language problems, but I know it's a war worth winning. I want them to be fluent in both languages and both traditions, as well. When I try to read a book or watch a movie, Olivia says, "in Spanish, yes, in Spanish."

Spanglish: One Language or a Mix of English and Spanish?

The ability of human beings to express themselves and communicate with others using articulated sound or other systems of signs is what is called language. To communicate we must have a common system that allows us to express an idea from one person to another, and to define this common system we use the word "language". The languages are changing according to each society. Let us bear in mind that a language is nothing more than a system of communication, verbal and written. Each language is subdivided by dialects, which responds to the different ways the language is spoken in different regions.

The official languages are constantly changing, either due to the incorporation of new words or due to the fact that peoples with different languages begin to converge regularly in the same place. These changes result in the language being modified or a new one emerging. For a long time, more and more Spanglish has been spoken about, which is nothing more than the result of a process similar to the one explained above. It arises from the mixture of people who have Spanish as their native language and speak English, or vice versa. Some people point to the 1940s and Puerto Ricoas the origin of this linguistic phenomenon. Although the greatest influence comes from the United States of America, where more than

40 million Spanish speakers live. There, parents try to keep their children from speaking Spanish, but the predominance of English, the official language, is so strong that it cannot be avoided using it, not even in the family language. Due to this, the combination of both languages has had to be assumed. On websites like Babbel, for example, you can find more information and references on the linguistic phenomenon of Spanglish.

Examples of Spanglish

There are several daily examples that can be heard of the mixture of both languages. Some common phrases are: "brother, tell me the time", to ask for the time; Are you ready?", alluding to whether you are ready; "Let's have lunch" , referring to going to lunch or eating; "Send an inbox" , which refers to sending an email. Other examples are simple words that resulted from combinations of a word in English and Spanish, such as: "parkear", which comes from parking in Spanish and park in English, and "sortear", which is the mixture of choosing in Spanish and sortin English. The language that predominates in the sentence will depend on the native language of the person in question. On the other hand, a case in which it is not possible to understand what the choice of one or another language depends on in everyday speech is that of bilingual subjects.

Where was speak

Puerto Rico including the United States of America are two of the countries that most influence this phenomenon, but they are not the only ones. Mexico, for example, on the border with the United States, has a constant exchange of citizens from both countries. For this reason, Mexico is also a linguistic exponent of this mixture of languages. The rest of the Latin American countries also have some influence, but to a lesser extent, since the language that continues to predominate is Spanish. In Spain, there are also some examples in everyday speech, although they are not really significant. Other English-speaking countries, such as England and Canada, have a very small population of people who speak Spanish, so you cannot speak of a true influence.

Future expansion

Many language specialists draw their conclusions about the expansion and development of this possible new language. Some claim that it will never become an official language, it will only contribute many words and phrases to both languages, but it will not go any further. Others, optimists regarding changes and evolution, believe that sooner or later it will end up imposing itself as a language that replaces the use of English and Spanish. In any case, we know that it exists and, with the arrival of new emigrants from Latin America to the United States, it will bring a result in terms of language that cannot be ignored in the future.

Bilingual people spontaneously mix languages quickly and agilely

How bilinguals control their two languages, how they switch from one to the other without apparent effort, and the neural mechanisms underlying these processes have been some of the most relevant questions in the field of cognitive science research on multilingualism recently.

However, most studies have focused on an unnatural implementation based on strict laboratory paradigms in which the change or alternation of languages occurs in response to a series of cues that tell bilinguals which language to use and when.

For example, in the presence of a specific flag accompanying a drawing, the name of that drawing must be said in one language, and if the flag changes, the language used to name the drawing must also change.

Predominance of one language

These studies generally show that it is easier for bilinguals to use one language than to use two to name objects. Despite this, the perception in the conversations that take place in the street in societies with the presence of several languages indicates something different, and points out that people mix languages voluntarily and with little effort.

A study, carried made by the Basque Center on Cognition, Brain and Language (BCBL) and the Nebrija University, shows that when bilinguals are free to use their two languages in the way they want, they can come to name the objects they see even more faster than when they are forced to use only one of their languages.

"One of the least valued but most interesting abilities of bilinguals is to switch between languages with apparent simplicity when the context allows it," says Angela De Bruin, researcher at the BCBL and author of the study.

Thus, this work shows that there is a strong tendency to alternate naturally between languages, contrary to what might have been expected from more purist perspectives on the use of the language. "This study shows the advantages of favoring the mixture of languages," says Jon Andoni Duñabeitia, a researcher at Nebrija University and co-author of the study.

An experiment with bilinguals

In the research, bilinguals from the Basque Country who spoke Spanish and Basque were asked to name images. The bilinguals had to name all the images in a single language (Basque or Spanish), or they could name the images in the language of their choice.

The first of the researchers' findings was that when the participants were allowed to use the language they wanted, the bilinguals very frequently switched between Spanish and Basque. "If we let bilinguals switch between their languages, they will do so more than we think," emphasizes De Bruin.

The second of the findings was also surprising. By measuring the time it took to name the images, the scientists found that bilinguals took less time to retrieve and produce the name of the images when they used two languages than when they were asked to use only one language. That is, not only did they voluntarily alternate between languages in a very frequent way, but this made their verbal productions faster.

These findings show that, contrary to what is often believed, the use of two languages does not always result in a negative effort, and depends on the context. On many occasions, the two languages of a bilingual are used in different contexts.

For example, a bilingual may use one language at school and another at home, or one language in their close family environment and another with friends. In these contexts, obviously, the bilingual needs to ensure that the appropriate language is used and that possible interference from the other language is adequately controlled.

Switch between languages

But in other situations in which a bilingual is surrounded by other bilinguals who also speak those languages fluently, the alternation between the two languages can be voluntary, free and positive. As De Bruin and his colleagues showed, in these types of contexts, the free use of the two languages can cost less effort and be more agile than the use of a single language.

Bilingual education systems often promote the use of only one language within the framework of a specific subject, and discourage children from mixing their languages. However, the results show that the mixture of languages is not a sign of poor use of the language nor does it denote a low level of competence in the languages. Quite the contrary, and as Duñabeitia defends, "the free use of both languages can help bilinguals to communicate more efficiently and with less effort, favoring linguistic inclusion".

Reasons why you should learn Spanish, the key to your personal growth

Here are more than 7,000 languages in the world, of which only 10% are spoken by more than 100,000 people; In other words, a large part of the world's population is focused on one of these languages.

So what makes Spanish stand out among these languages? Is Spanish really relevant among the many possibilities that exist for languages to learn?

Of course, learning a language will always be a relevant project in the life of any person, but Spanish retains a special place among all languages. Currently more than 570 million people in the world speak Spanish (not only in Spanish-speaking countries).

But it is not only because of the number of people who speak it, you should also consider that although Mandarin is the most widely spoken language and English retains a large number of speakers, Spanish is the only one of all these languages that retains a process of expansion, that is to say that more and more people speak it; meanwhile, Mandarin and English have been decreasing in scope, that is, fewer and fewer people are interested in learning it.

If you still do not feel that Spanish is the best option, do not worry, in this article Superprof tells you what are the reasons that make Spanish a good language to learn in Colombia and how you can get the most out of your Spanish classes to foreign.

Explore the world and discover new countries thanks to Spanish

Whenever we think about the reasons for learning a language, this is one of the first motivations; Traveling is a pleasure that, even if it costs us a lot, is always worth it.

When we want to start a trip we must take into account what things we should take with us, prepare suitcases, find a good hotel and tickets, but if we really want to enjoy the whole experience of a trip it is very important to know their language.

It can be frustrating not to understand the people around us, looking for something as simple as a good restaurant or a taxi becomes a challenge. Taking Spanish classes for foreigners is a way to solve this problem since you can go to visit Spanish-speaking countries and immerse yourself in their culture.

Expansion of Spanish throughout the world

Throughout history the discovery of America has been one of the most important events for humanity, it was the birth of a society born of oppression and the mixture of cultures. It all started with the arrival of Christopher Columbus to the territory on a small island in the Bahamas in the year 1492.

From that moment onwards, colonization campaigns were carried out throughout the entire continent by England, France, Italy, Portugal and the most important, the Spanish, which predominated the majority of the territory. Thanks to this, the Spanish language spread throughout the Americas.

As in America, Spain began to arrive in new lands; In Africa there were colonies from this European country and even today in countries like Equatorial Guinea there are a large number of people who speak Spanish. There are also people who speak Spanish in the Philippines as a result of the Colonization that ended in the 19th century. In other words, if you start your Spanish classes for foreigners, you can get to know the whole world.

Attractive tourist destinations that you can take advantage of thanks to Spanish for foreigners

If you feel ready to put your ELE (Spanish for Foreigners) classes into practice

Although it is true that Latin America is not the only place where Spanish is spoken (There is also Spain, Equatorial Guinea and other territories divided by Africa, Asia and Europe); The American continent has the largest number of Spanish-speaking countries in the world, therefore making it one of the most important destinations when it comes to learning Spanish for foreigners.

- Mexico: It is a country recognized throughout the world for its culture, its music and its food; Its beautiful beaches in places like Cancun or Acapulco are a favorite destination for tourists when it comes to learning concerning Hispanic culture and therefore practicing Spanish for foreigners.
- Spain: The motherland of the Spanish language never ceases to be the first Spanish-speaking destination visited, among its greatest attractions are the architecture of its cathedrals, the aqueduct of Segovia and even its natural parks; a cultural and historical paradise where to learn Spanish for foreigners.
- Peru: thousands of years ago it was the home of the Inca civilization and the vestiges of it are precisely the most attractive, destinations such as Cusco or Machu Picchu reflect the best of their architecture, in addition to the beautiful landscapes that you can find in this South American country. .

- Chile: Another pearl of Latin America, it has the four seasons, amazing landscapes and emblematic places such as Easter Island and Viña del Mar where world-class musical events are held. You can take advantage of your holidays to put your ELE classes into practice.

- Colombia: A country with varied climates throughout its extension, it has famous beaches such as those of San Andrés or if you are more of an adventure you can visit the Colombian Amazon and its incredible diversity. You can also learn Spanish in many academies that exist throughout the country.

Working for the world speaking Spanish

Another of the most practical applications of learning a language is work, having a professional projection and expanding our opportunities when looking for a new job.

If what you want is to be able to fulfill your dream of traveling around the world without the need to stop working, Spanish is precisely the language that can help you achieve your goal. The fact that there are various people around the world who are Spanish speakers gives us a notion of the importance of the Spanish language in the business and work environment.

Taking into account that in all corners of the planet we can find people who speak Spanish and even groups and entire communities that handle this language, it is important for many people to learn it and also dedicate a special space to Spanish.

Become an ELE teacher and work on any continent

As we have already mentioned, Spanish is a language that is growing in demand, its stability is unique and instead of being left behind it has come to occupy an important place in countries that do not recognize it as an official language.

If you want to learn Spanish, you can become a Spanish teacher for foreigners in many countries. In Asian countries such as China, Japan or South Korea there is a high demand for people seeking to learn and master the Spanish language; there are places where you can earn up to $25 per hour teaching the Spanish language.

But what does it take to become an ELE teacher?

If your origin is a Latin country or maybe Spain you already have an advantage, you speak Spanish perfectly; But it is not enough to have practice, theory is important. You must learn:

- Semantics
- Orthography
- Grammar structure
- Punctuation

Pedagogical techniques for teaching

Each of these studies is the complement you need to become a good ELE teacher, it is not mandatory to have a course or a special study but it is important that you can give a boost to your work as ELE; It's like any profession, the more specialty you have, the easier it is for you to get a good job.

Spanish and its importance for international business

In an era of globalization and international connection, it is important to maintain good communication with everyone, languages are therefore essential when it comes to having clear trade conditions between countries and companies.

If you are already a professional in administration or in another business profession, Spanish opens doors for you due to the international processes that you can handle with any of the 21 countries that currently recognize the Spanish language as official; It is true that English is the language of business, but being bilingual gives you the possibility of expanding your horizons towards internationalization.

Take your ELE (Spanish for Foreigners) classes to enrich your curriculum and thus be able to find better job opportunities in many countries. If you wish, you can find good options to learn Spanish in Colombia or in other Latin American countries.

Some reasons to study Spanish in Colombia

One of the priorities that we must take into account when learning a new language is to know its use and there is nothing better than doing it while you are in a country where the language is spoken.

Immersing yourself in a place where you can even learn some idioms or expressions helps you master your understanding of Spanish. But if there are so many countries to learn Spanish, why take Spanish classes for foreigners in Colombia?

Cities where you can learn Spanish in Colombia

If what you want is to focus on learning, it is better that you can access one of the academies that offer Spanish courses for foreigners in the most important cities of the country: Bogotá, Medellín, Cali, Barranquilla, Cúcuta and Cartagena.

If you wish, you can consider the following points before choosing where you want to start your Spanish classes for foreigners:

- City climate
- Cost of living and studies
- Closeness and mobility facilities
- Housing options
- Regional culture

Study Spanish in Bogotá

Although it is not the only city where there are high quality academies and study centers, Bogotá has made its way throughout the continent to the first destination to which people who want to take Spanish classes for foreigners go, surpassing to other popular destinations like Mexico or Argentina.

Why study in Bogotá:

- Because it's the most important business centers in Latin America and you can practice the language at a professional level
- Because it is well recognized as part of the city where Spanish is spoken with greater fluency and number of words.
- Because it has the least pronounced accent in the world, it is easier to understand
- Because it has excellent study centers and also a good quality of life without exceeding the possibilities of paying for the stay

Another very good source of learning Spanish for foreigners that can be found in the city is the number of personalized teachers of the language. You can find more than 1,500 options on pages such as Superprof with prices starting at $ 15,000 Colombian pesos per hour ($ 4 Dollars).

Support your learning process in Colombian culture

When we are interested in a language it is normal that this interest is impregnated with curiosity to know more about its origin and its use.

With more than 21 Spanish-speaking countries, the variety of customs and cultures that you can discover are abysmal. Some of them are more widespread and known all over the world such as the Mexican or the Spanish; but places like Colombia have thousands of experiences to offer you to improve your level of Spanish.

Colombia has throughout its territory so many parties, fairs and carnivals that it is impossible to attend all of them in a year; it takes at least 5 years in a row to achieve it.

It is a country that has 12 recognized departments, 5 regions and hundreds of traditions that you can get to know. Getting in contact with native Spanish speakers will always be the easiest way to get to understand the use of the language and improve your pronunciation and use of vocabulary.

Some of the advantages that you can find in Colombia to learn Spanish for foreigners thanks to its culture are:

- The diversity of cultures adds more uses to words and a number of words to learn
- Colombia has many resources that you can use to improve all dimensions of the language (speaking, writing, listening and reading)

- The warmth of the people helps you create bonds of friendship that allow you to practice Spanish for foreigners
- Due to the number of parties, festivals and carnivals you can attend multicultural events that teach you a little more about Latin culture
- Dare to know Colombia and enjoy the diversity of its people and the beauty of the national territory.

All The Information You Need About Spanish As A Foreign Language

Teaching Spanish as a foreign language in language classes for non-Spanish speaking students is totally different from a Spanish language course in Spain. Learning Spanish as a foreign language is totally like learning Russian, German, English or French as a first or second language.

It is about teaching Spanish to those foreigners who have not had that opportunity before.

What is the ELE?

The acronym ELE means "Spanish as a Foreign Language". These are Spanish classes taught to students who have a different mother tongue, especially immigrants, tourists, indigenous people, refugees and anyone else who has to learn it for work, business, diplomacy or cultural curiosity. The acronym is opposed to ELM, which means "Spanish as a Mother Language."

The mother tongue is the language we learn during early childhood and the one spoken by native speakers.

Little history of the ELE

The teaching of a foreign language is a question that arises from the 18th century with the different travels and geographical discoveries. The traditional methodology appears just at that moment and will be used until the middle of the 19th century. It will be a method based on grammar and the translation of texts from the original language into Spanish. Oral expression has no place and Spanish is seen as a cultural contribution, spoken by many of the most influential figures of that time.

From the year 1870, the direct method appeared, much less rigid. The original language, used until now to translate the terms, has no place on this occasion. Spanish is used throughout the class. Oral begins to be an option and grammar is studied through deduction.

Between the 1920s and 1960s, we moved to an active methodology, where traditional and direct methodologies are combined: the student is the one at the center of learning Spanish. The mother tongue is allowed again in class.

In the 1950s, the structural-global-audiovisual method (SGAV) appeared which is based on three principles: communication, dialogue and image.

The limits of this method are that it allows you to communicate with natives in a much faster way, but not to understand them when they speak to each other or to understand what the media is saying.

In the 1970s, the communicative approach was developed with the arrival of adult migrants, which sought to respond to their needs.

The method used today is based on the notion of homework. Priority is given to the interaction between the student and the teacher, but also between the students in the class.

What are your goals?

The objective of ELE is always the same: to facilitate the integration of students in the host country.

Students can vary and teachers must adapt according to the type of student body:

- political refugees,
- Erasmus students,
- precocious audience,
- schoolchildren,
- teenagers,
- adults, etc.

Spanish can seem difficult for a foreign student, especially when the mother tongue has nothing to do with Latin. In these cases, you will require great motivation.

Here are some useful Spanish expressions to get you started, translated into English and French.

- Courtesy forms
- Good morning / Bonjour / Hello,
- Hello / Salut / Hi,
- Good evening / Bonsoir / Good evening,
- Goodbye / Au revoir / Good bye,
- Goodbye / A demain / See you tomorrow,
- Thank you / Merci / Thank you,
- You're welcome / De rien / You're welcome,
- Sorry / Excusez-moi / I'm sorry,
- Enchanted / a / Enchanté / Nice to meet you,
- How are you? / Comment allez-vous? / How are you?,

Well, thank you / Très bien, merci / I'm fine, thank you.

Presentation formulas

My name is ... / Je m'appelle... / My name is...,

As it is called? / Comment vous appelez-vous? / What's your name?

I am French / English / Spanish / Je suis français / anglais / espagnol / I'm French / English / Spanish,

I am 25 years old / J'ai 25 years old / I'm 25 years old.

In this more complete article, we will offer you more expressions in Spanish to be able to ask for the signs and move around the city, order in a restaurant or reserve a room in a hotel.

ELE: expressions in Spanish that you should know

To be able to work in Spain, it is better to learn Spanish. For this, there is nothing better than ELE courses that start from scratch or that seek to improve the level of the language.

How can you work in Spain if you are a foreigner?

I am a citizen of the European Economic Area (EEA)

The citizens belonging to the EEA (28 members of the European Union, Norway, Iceland and Liechtenstein) can work freely in Spain provided they have a passport or a valid identity because they have the same rights as Spanish citizens.

Outside the EEA, the process is more complex. It will be necessary to obtain a work permit from the Spanish authorities (residence permit).

Foreign students that wish to work in Spain

Also, you may want to study in Spain and work in order to pay for your stay and classes. In that case, it will be enough to have a valid residence card and be registered in an official educational center.

Citizens from the EEA have certain privileges, as they will not have to apply for a temporary work permit, while those from third countries do.

Of course, if you work in Spain, you can study the language at the same time. Coming to Spain without learning the language will not allow you to easily access a job.

Create your own business in Spain when you are a foreigner

If you want to join a company in Spain or become a partner of a company, you will have no problem because there are no limits. Of course, EU citizens have more privileges, as long as the country acceded before May 2004 or belongs to the EEA (Iceland, Norway, Liechtenstein or Switzerland).

What are the characteristics of Spanish as a Foreign Language?

Learning Spanish in Spain is usually more attractive than learning it in language schools or at the Instituto Cervantes, but how can you learn Spanish as a foreign language in Spain?

A well-organized course

A teacher of Spanish that's of foreign language need to undergo university training before teaching ELE and before even starting to teach the first class, they must have certain information to be able to prepare it:

- The duration of the course;
- the level of the students (initial, intermediate, advanced);
- the age of the students;
- the origin (what is the mother tongue of the students);
- the objectives;
- the material conditions;
- the number of students.

In general, the communicative approach is preferred because more time is given to speaking from the first class thanks to the different exercises.

The ELE is framed within the Common European Framework of Reference for Languages (CEFR) and must achieve a balance between the five skills that must be worked on:

- written comprehension,
- oral comprehension,
- written expression,
- continuous oral expression,
- oral expression in interaction.

Of course, the goal of the teacher is to advance students through fun exercises, but also to create group cohesion that encourages and encourages students to work.

Progress in ELE classes

On the first day, the teacher must evaluate the level of each student in order to adapt and prepare their classes in relation to the results: first, because they do not know the students; second, because students can come from different classes and levels; and finally, because it is a good way to really know the abilities of the students.

Progress in your level of Spanish may take longer than you expected, but this progress is individual and independent of the group, so the teacher will carry out a personalized and individualized monitoring of each student.

Also, keep in mind that the progression is not linear, but there are ups and downs. The classes will be more or less easy depending on the students and their abilities.

Spanish as a foreign language classes are different from Spanish classes at high school or university

In Spanish classes for high school or university students, the focus will be on grammar, vocabulary, spelling and critical thinking training. However, in French classes for foreigners, the focus will be on learning to speak a language. The classes and exercises will aim to learn to function in everyday life in order to better integrate in Spain.

ELE teaching focuses on learning Spanish by foreigners (Spanish for foreigners), either in Spain or anywhere else in the world.

To begin with, it is possible to learn Spanish online by studying some typical expressions, such as courtesy formulas.

Working in Spain for a foreigner is different depending on whether they are an EEA citizen or not. Each case will have to be studied.

Progress in your level of Spanish, as in any language, will depend on the motivation of each student, but also on their abilities.

If you live in Catalonia, do not hesitate to look for Spanish courses for foreigners in Barcelona on Superprof.

How To Learn Spanish

In Spain When You Are A Foreigner Or A Foreigner, Learning The Cervantes Language Can Be Essential, Especially To Live In Spain

How can you do it easily and improve your language level effectively?

Spanish classes for adults,

Tutorials

Websites,

Mobile applications to learn ELE...

With or without a budget, we are going to take a tour of the different solutions to learn to speak Spanish when you are a foreigner.

How can you master the language to speak Spanish fluently on a daily basis? Discover our tips and improve your language skills in Spanish.

Elena

SPANISH TEACHER FOR FOREIGNERS

4.88

4.88

(10)

$ 50,000 / h

1 a free class!

Discover all the teachers

Javier

SPANISH TEACHER FOR FOREIGNERS

5.00

5.00

(3)

$ 25,000 / h

1 a free class!

Discover all the teachers

William Tenesor

SPANISH TEACHER FOR FOREIGNERS

5.00

5.00

(4)

$ 25,000 / h

1 a free class!

Discover all the teachers

Nesly melissa

SPANISH TEACHER FOR FOREIGNERS

5.00

5.00

(8)

$ 45,000 / h

1 a free class!

Discover all the teachers

Daniel felipe

SPANISH TEACHER FOR FOREIGNERS

5.00

5.00

(6)

$ 25,000 / h

1 a free class!

Discover all the teachers

Sandra

SPANISH TEACHER FOR FOREIGNERS

5.00

5.00

(5)

$ 30,000 / h

1 a free class!

Discover all the teachers

cease

SPANISH TEACHER FOR FOREIGNERS

5.00

5.00

(8)

$ 38,000 / h

1 a free class!

Discover all the teachers

Angie

SPANISH TEACHER FOR FOREIGNERS

4.94

4.94

(4)

$ 12,000 / h

1 a free class!

Discover all the teachers

Is it possible to learn Spanish when you are a foreigner?

When discussing foreign languages that are difficult to learn, students often mention:

- The Arab,
- the Chinese,
- the Japanese,
- the German.

Actually, it all depends on the linguistic roots of the person! Because although it is often said that Spanish is a particularly difficult language to learn, it is usually easier for those who speak a Romance language than for others. Therefore, the French, the Portuguese, or the Italians can learn to speak Spanish much faster.

However, Spanish has several major difficulties:

- a dense conjugation,
- two genders (male and female) that make students sometimes confuse,
- a grammar that most Spaniards do not even know by heart,
- And a very rich vocabulary!

Despite its difficulties, obviously, everyone can learn to speak Spanish. And why not take Spanish classes for foreigners to achieve it?

Spanish classes for foreigners: free solutions

If you need an accompaniment in your learning of Spanish, then the most convenient thing is to take classes in a language school or private classes of

Spanish as a foreign language. The only disadvantage is that these classes are paid.

Free ELE solutions

Why don't you take ELE classes in an association?

Depending on the situation, you may not have the budget to finance Spanish classes and make rapid progress. In this case, even without spending anything, there are solutions to take Spanish classes for free.

You can contact the associations that offer Spanish classes for foreigners. They are usually the only structures that carry out free Spanish learning workshops. The associations work thanks to the help of volunteers, who have the necessary skills to work as Spanish teachers.

Their missions are varied, but the associations that deal with the foreign public most of the time carry out Spanish language workshops or literacy classes to facilitate the integration of foreigners. They also participate in the fight against illiteracy since the language barrier is a great obstacle to creating a social bond but also to integrating professionally.

To take Spanish classes in an association, you have two possibilities. You can contact with:

- The main national or international associations such as FEDELE (Spanish Federation of Associations of Schools of Spanish for

Foreigners) and ASELE (Association for the Teaching of Spanish as a Foreign Language),

- Local associations. If there are associations in your city that offer classes in Spanish as a foreign language, you can inquire at the town hall.

If you are in Spain for postgraduate studies, you can also ask your center to find out if they offer ELE classes for foreign students. There are many universities and colleges that run workshops for international students. The goal is to better integrate them and help them improve their language practice so that they will be successful in their academic year.

Are you looking for a Spanish teacher course for foreigners online?

Can you take Spanish classes for foreigners online?

One of the most accessible solutions is the online ELE lessons. Many websites, often free, offer lessons to learn a new language independently and self-taught.

This solution can be very effective, as long as you take it seriously and study Spanish with effort and regularity.

ELE web pages

To take free Spanish lessons, a good solution is the websites specialized in language learning.

For this training to be productive, it is important to choose the website that allows you to study Spanish in the best possible way. Therefore, you must take into account certain criteria:

- Your language level: take a Spanish level test to find out what your level is (beginner, intermediate or advanced level). You can find Spanish lessons online that adapt to your progress in learning Spanish. Some sites are designed to get started in the language (level A1 or A2), while others offer didactic supports to reach the intermediate level (B1 or B2).
- The learning mode: which methodology is best for you (practice through games to learn Spanish, lessons, and exercises by topic, visual or audio aids ...)?
- Your needs: do you want to improve your knowledge of Spanish to travel, pursue higher education in Spain, work in a Spanish-speaking country...?
- Follow-up: some sites offer personalized online classes with individualized follow-up (correction of exercises, tips ...).

These websites have many advantages. You will be able to study all aspects of the language (written comprehension, oral comprehension, written expression, and oral expression), and they offer a variety of supports to more easily learn grammar, spelling, conjugation, vocabulary, pronunciation...

Videos, podcasts,

Written supports,

Complete lessons with interactive exercises,

Lessons of culture and civilization,

Vocabulary cards by topic and idiomatic expressions.

Thanks to voice recognition, you can also learn to pronounce the most difficult words in Spanish correctly and practice intonation.

Among the sites that you can use to learn Spanish, we can mention some very useful, specially adapted to learn ELE:

- On-Spanish. The page has many exercises and study materials to help you improve quickly that you can access for free by registering on the page. You can also take their tests to check your progress and, in addition, they organize different webinars.

- Learn Spanish. This page contains a collection of hundreds of free exercises to learn Spanish on the Internet: grammar, vocabulary, songs, reading, stories, videos, podcasts, etc. In addition, it contains a list of links to exercises in Spanish.
- BBC - Languages - Spanish. BBC Spanish classes, starting from beginner level, with grammar, dictionaries, lessons, reports, audios, games ... It also has resources for Spanish teachers.
- Learn Spanish. You will find vocabulary and grammar notes for ELE students and a series of links to other pages. In addition, they have a section, adapted for students, dedicated to gastronomy with recipes, expressions, and vocabulary.

You can also learn Spanish with platforms such as Duolingo, Babbel, or Mosalingua, which are sites specialized in learning modern languages, including Spanish.

Spanish Classes For Foreigners: The Best Applications

Online lesson sites for learning Spanish are useful, but to optimize your learning, you can also download tools that allow you to practice anywhere and at any time of the day, according to your possibilities.

With the mobile applications of Spanish as a foreign language, you can easily practice even outside the home. You can also download complementary applications that will be very helpful in your day today:

- A dictionary of Spanish,
- An app for conjugation,
- A voice translator,
- An application to work grammar,

Apart from the mobile applications that offer Spanish classes and exercises, you will need other complementary applications.

When you are a foreigner, and you arrive in a country with only a few notions of the language, it is not easy to adapt to the new environment, discover new customs, but above all communicate to go shopping, ask for directions, introduce yourself and have a conversation...

In this context, even if you take Spanish classes for foreigners, feel free to use all the apps that will help you in your daily situations. Thanks to these practical tools, you will be able to take complete and clear Spanish lessons to learn at your own pace and improve your skills a little more every day.

Among the applications dedicated to Spanish as a foreign language, you can, for example, download for free:

- Busuu: a very interesting application in terms of social learning and the large community of Spanish speakers who use it. In addition to the very clear and complete lessons, you can communicate live with native speakers ... Free conversation classes!
- Rosetta Stone is another of the star apps and one of the oldest. The fundamental difference is that translations into English or any other language are not used. The idea is to learn Spanish in Spanish. You will be able to learn to speak, read and understand Spanish.
- Memrise. This fun application will allow you to develop your vocabulary simply with flashcards and mnemonic techniques based on repetition. In addition, the application is very entertaining, and you can watch videos made by native speakers of the language.
- Spanish Pronunciation. You can practice and then improve your pronunciation in Spanish with this simple application. It works offline, so you can practice anywhere. You will learn Spanish pronunciation by listening to how words are pronounced and repeating them.

The unique method to learn a language is to do a total immersion, but it is necessary to benefit from good language learning to progress more quickly.

Whether taking Spanish classes in Spain or taking online lessons, it is essential to practice daily and enjoy language immersion in the country to perfect the language.

Last tips to reach your goals:

- Practice regularly,
- Do exercises to acquire automatisms,
- Review your vocabulary cards daily,
- Read in Spanish,
- Speak as much as possible...

Repetition is key to success if you want to learn to speak Spanish fluently.

How To Organize Notebooks To Learn Languages Effectively.

To achieve that magnificent task of learning languages, one thing that you cannot miss is a notebook where you can practice and write down everything new you learn.

Now a blank notebook can seem a bit overwhelming. What to write Where to begin? I confess it happens to all of us!

That is why you have a better idea of what to write in your language notebook, below; I share a structure that you can use for your notebooks.

In addition to helping you organize, this structure is based on the best language acquisition methods shared by polyglots like Gabriel Wyner (author of the famous book Fluent Forever), language teachers I have met around the world, and by my own experience. Studying languages.

Benefits of having a language notebook

Having a language notebook is key during your language learning process. Since languages are made up of words, there is no better way to learn and memorize them than by writing them down!

Besides being key, having a language notebook brings you several benefits:

- Helps you enter a world where you write, read and think in your new language
- It gives you your own space for expression and connection with your learning process.
- It enables us to get track of your progress in learning languages.
- Helps you keep your notes organized
- You make sure you learn the language step by step and cohesively.

Structure for your language notebook

The following structure is based on the four steps to learn languages that I tell you on the blog. It is a recommended structure, but you can add more things if you consider that they will help you study the language you want to learn.

- Goals
- Alphabet
- Vocabulary
- Verbs
- Grammar
- Useful phrases
- Diary

1. Goals

The first section of your notebook is dedicated to writing down your goals and your motivation for learning. This will ensure that your process with your language of interest is more successful, and you do not lose sight of your motivation and what you want to achieve.

Do you want to learn languages to study for a master's degree in another country? Or maybe you want to learn a language to be able to communicate with new international friends? Whatever objective you have, you must set a clear goal and write it down.

Once you write your overall goal, set goals that are actionable, preferably one with a measurable number. For example, learn five words a day listen to 30 minutes of an audiobook or write a paragraph 5 days a week.

2. Alphabet

Now that you got your goals defined, the next section of your notebook will be dedicated to learning the alphabet and the pronunciation of each letter (or character).

In this process, you will be familiarizing yourself with the new language's sounds and how to pronounce them, including how to write them.

Write the vowels on a sheet and the consonants on another and accompany each one with its pronunciation. To do this, you can use the IPA (International Phonetic Alphabetic) and write phonetically how each one is pronounced.

As you learn the written alphabet, you will learn how to pronounce it. For this, you can:

- Learn the International Phonetic Alphabet (IPA)
- Find videos on YouTube with native speakers who explain and show you how to pronounce each letter.
- Use apps and websites like Forvo and Memrise to sharpen listening

3. Vocabulary

If you are getting from scratch, start by learning and writing down the most common and most frequently used words in the language. To do this, Google "Most Common Words in (the language you are learning)." This way,, you can lay the groundwork and learn words that will help you communicate and are commonly used.

Among the vocabulary that you will learn are nouns, adjectives, adverbs, articles, pronouns, and prepositions.

An example of basic words that you would start to learn in a new language are:

- Weekdays
- Months of the year
- Colors
- Numbers
- Members of the family
- Seasons of the year

If you already have a more advanced level but want to learn more specific vocabulary, you can also look for common words according to your area of interest (travel, work, hobbies) and write them down.

4. Verbs

The next thing you will learn is verbs. Learn the most common verbs or those you need to accomplish the goal you defined at the beginning.

Although verbs are part of the vocabulary, it is important to have them separated by a very important aspect: conjugation.

The conjugation of verbs can be given according to:

The subject who is acting (I, you, she/he, they/they, we, you)

The time when the action happens (past, present, future)

Write down in your notebook the verbs with their conjugation according to the subject and the time. This will help you later give context to each action.

5. Grammar

When you have learned vocabulary and verbs, the next thing you want to know is how to connect them correctly to build sentences. This is where you will start documenting the grammar of your new language.

It is not an overwhelming section for you and on the contrary you learn effectively, always write an example next to all grammar rules.

Instead of memorizing a rule or pattern on its own, memorize the example. Try to write an example that relates to your personal life that will make memorization easier and help you stay motivated.

6. Useful phrases

Set aside a section of your notebook to jot down a list of useful phrases and recurring sayings. This will be very helpful in taking the step of speaking. You can write down the most basic phrases, such as "My name is..." or write down the ones you consider necessary according to your goals (travel, work, hobbies).

Try to understand the grammar of what you are saying and the pronunciation.

7. Diary

Set aside a section of your notebook for writing practice. The writing exercise trains you to put the patterns you have learned into practice and turn them into stories.

Write about a topic/title that you are passionate about to make writing a fun activity. You can write your opinions on a topic, retell your day, write a story, imagine what the country is like where you would like to go, or write about anything else you like a lot!

And there you have the structure to organize your language notebook!

To help you with your learning goal, I am creating a ready printable practical notebook with organized templates and following a strategic order so that learning a language is easy and fun.

You can print the notebook or use it digitally on a tablet. It will be useful for whatever language you are learning: English, French, German, Korean,

Japanese… Once you use it for one language, you can use it for any other.

Online Resources For Learning A Language From Home

The home language learning odyssey can be lengthy. Learning a foreign language requires commitment and persistence. However, learning another language has its benefits, including getting more job opportunities.

Knowing many languages is nothing new. You will have merits when applying for a job compared to those who don't know languages.

It will help you communicate with other people, you can talk to more clients and companies, and it will improve your chances of getting a better job.

How many job opportunities have you noticed for bilingual candidates? Surely

What language to learn now? All these diverse languages Hundreds of languages to pick from.

Languages that have stronger job prospects certainly exist. Here you can see an infographic about the most widely spoken and studied languages across the globe. This other article details the most demanded languages to work with.

Tricks to accelerate your language learning

A language learned quickly is just a basic one. How can this be done? To speed up your language learning, follow these steps:

- Start with the most used terms

Use only the most important words. Bathroom, eating, talking, paying Next, you can learn all the lesser-used words (animal names, technical words, etc.).

- Commonize your terms

Do an hour-long practice every day in the language by listening, watching, reading, and writing.

- inform natives

Nothing more instructive than conversing with locals. This is the only path. You can master the language you like by learning abroad, or you can use apps, Skype, and other forums. Make use of these language-exchange online portals.

Look up the phrase in the dictionary

Dictionaries are for learning new words. Never be without it. Now it is much simpler with smartphones that have dictionaries built into them or apps such as Google Translate.

Think in another language

It may sound strange but thinking in another language is a good resource for learning another language.

Do not be afraid

Many times you do not speak another language for fear of failure, not pronouncing it well, or being ashamed. Don't worry; no one is born knowing.

Tools to learn a language from home

You can learn languages by traveling overseas, or at a language school where you speak to other people. per learning environment is advantageous

There are various free and online options for learning a language from home.

All the time with ABA films from the UK

- a fun way to learn a language
- I use LiveMocha.
- using Google Translation
- simple
- simple
- English BBC
- mem
- trouble
- memorization app
- a multi-lingual club
- phrase exchange
- Culture of Transparency
- all-knowing

Forvo Technology has changed everything by allowing us access to infinite energy. Using free education to your benefit.

You may not understand and master a language in a day, but you have the time to devote to learning it.

"Learning A Language Requires Motivation And Time, And The Key Is To Listen And Read"

Spain usually always appears in the last positions in the knowledge of languages. Why is it so hard for us Spaniards to learn a new language, and why does it even cause us anxiety?

There are several reasons. In Spanish, as in Japanese, there are few vowel sounds. So, in the head of a Spaniard, there are only those sounds; there are no more. Another reason is the dubbing of series or movies. In Sweden, as is also the case in other countries such as Croatia, films are broadcast in their original version, and that is very important when learning a new language.

What are the advantages for a child of watching cartoons in their original version?

The brain becomes more flexible; the child acquires new sounds and more ways of saying things. In addition, they get used to the uncertainty of what they are hearing. There will be many words that they will not understand, but the child will move on and will not stop to think that he has just heard something that he does not understand. It is important to accept when you start to learn a language that you cannot understand everything. Uncertainty is a very important factor in learning a language.

Does genetics play a role in language proficiency?

No, language learning is a matter of attitude and time. Lomb Kató, a prominent Hungarian polyglot, had a formula. He said that learning a language was equal to attitude and time divided by the entire negative (frustration, fear, inhibition ...).

Here we are used to seeing footballers from Eastern Europe or former Baltic republics who quickly learn Spanish and speak it well; however, it costs the British and Dutch much more. Is there any explanation?

In Canada, we have many ice hockey players from Russia or the Czech Republic who in one or two years speak English very well and with little accent. But also teachers from these countries who have lived in Canada for 20 years and who continue to have a strong accent. Athletes usually want to participate in their city and their team, and learning the language well is an attitude. The British may think that they don't need to learn Spanish because everyone speaks English. This may also be the case for the Dutch, who tend to speak English very well.

One study ranks Swedes, Latvians, and Danes among the most polyglot Europeans. Why do you think this is happening?

Probably because few people speak those languages.

Can you learn a language well at 60?

I learn faster now that I am 74 years old than I was 15 because I am more motivated and more confident. I have the feeling that I speak Spanish better now than I did twenty years ago, and that is because I have not stopped learning new languages , and I have accustomed my brain to new sounds. Thanks to that fitness (gymnastics) of the brain, language learning improves.

What is the right age to learn a new language?

The younger, the better; the more flexible our brain is. From the age of 12, it becomes more rigid.

Are you in favor of the child starting to learn a new language in kindergarten when he is barely speaking?

Of course, the more exposure and listening to a language a child receives, even at that age, the better. In Montreal, I meet a four-year-old boy with a Chinese father and a Japanese mother who has a Mexican au pair. He speaks Japanese with the mother, Chinese with the father, Spanish with the au pair, and English is learned on television. It may be confusing for some children at first, but they end up mastering those languages.

Here in most institutes, there are only three hours a week of English or a foreign language. Is that enough?

It's not much, really. Also, the way languages are often taught badly because they start with grammar. If I have no experience with a language or insufficient experience, all these grammatical explanations do not make sense because I will not be able to apply them. You have to start learning a language by listening and reading. Learning a language involves accustoming the ear, once this makes sense, for example, studying a table of conjugations. I will also be more receptive because I will already have a point of reference.

However, in classrooms, there is often little space for listening...

Professor Stephen Krashen, one of the leaders in the study and acquisition of languages, says that in class, it would be good to read and listen, leaving aside the grammar rules, but parents and administrators do not see it the same. In Canada, in the English system, children study French from the second year for thirty minutes every day, but twelve years later, they do not master the language.

And why does it happen?

They are poorly motivated. In Canada, it is an obligation, and everything that is mandatory is bad.

Is the way languages are taught in school bad?

The formula with which the teacher insists his students answer a series of questions or know how to utilize the language correctly after each lesson is wrong because the acquisition of a language is made slowly through input. There are contents that take time to be assimilated and others that do it faster. It is not good to read a story and then ask students about the meaning of words they do not understand. It is essential that the language enters the head; although there are doubts about vocabulary, it does not matter.

And how do you get the language to penetrate?

Through listening and reading, you learn better than through exams, theoretical explanations, and the traditional learning system. An example: in the Canadian province of New Brunswick, which has French and English as official languages, there were not enough resources for a small town to be able to hire teachers to teach English, and it was decided to offer some students audiobooks with them. that they could follow the contents that they found most interesting. After two years, these students were found to read and speak better than those who had followed traditional teaching with teachers.

Advice Starts Learning A New Language From Scratch.

Let him listen to (movies, series, songs ...) and read a lot in that language. It is good to hear stories over and over but from different points of view. The brain wants repetition but also newness; if; if not, it gets tired. If you try to work hard to learn the same content until you can master it, the learning process becomes less and less effective.

What should the administration do to improve the command of a language?

The main thing is not to dub movies or series and offer programs in their original version.

Should a government invest money so that a language does not disappear?

It is a pity that a language dies, but there are more serious problems. If the people who speak it don't want to keep it, what can you do! It is inevitable that languages will die, although I believe that currently, the conditions to maintain languages that few people speak are more favorable than ever. In Canada, there are indigenous languages in which the government wants to invest money so that they are not lost. But I think the best thing would be to find people who speak this language, transcribe their conversations, and create a library of resources that allows whoever wants to learn that language.

Why has Esperanto not triumphed as a universal language?

It is a language without country, cuisine, or music... So it is not very attractive, and people perceive it as a hobby.

What's the point of being a polyglot in the world of tech translators?

When you learn a language, the inhabitants who speak it become more alive, more real, less stereotyped; In addition, we learn not only the language but also the culture of that country. The experience of learning a new language allows you to connect with the person who speaks it, with the history of that country. No automatic translator gives you that pleasure.

Three Ways To Help Your Brain Learn A Language

I know that there are steps you can take to overcome a learning challenge. My best advice for making the brain master a foreign language is:

1. Create a sense of urgency

One of the most common excuses when learning a language? Lack of time.

After a full day at school or work, filling your brain with information, your brain may refuse to learn a language for one simple reason: it doesn't want to expend more energy.

So what can you do?

Join a class with more people

Any kind of class. Online, face-to-face, or a weekend workshop. The point is to have someone to help you keep up. Being committed to showing your progress to other people, especially classmates and teachers, will give you some healthy pressure.

Keep track of progress ... and share it.

Have you ever thought of recording audio or video to record your progress? How about sharing your latest essay, letter, or expression on social media? There is a large language learning community on Twitter and Facebook; you will also find several groups that will help you continue studying and sharing tips.

Don't give your brain a chance to escape the language.

Listening to songs on the way to school or work, watching Netflix movies or shows on the weekends, reading a magazine over breakfast, or posting on social media in the language you're learning are all great ways to get serious about your studies.

You can also put notes on the objects surrounding you in the language you are learning; thus, you will be in constant contact with the vocabulary. The point is to send the message to your brain that you should use that language because it is the one that surrounds you.

2. Make your learning as personal as possible

Our brains tend to forget things that we don't need or find interesting. Most of us complain about having a poor memory and not remembering new vocabulary, for example, but it is natural due to the vast amount of information that our brains grapple with every day.

Your mission? Trick your brain into believing that these words in another language are important and necessary.

Use your photos

The next time you make a study card for the word "dog" in English, French or German, keep in mind that it is easier for your brain to remember the word if you take a picture of your dog and use it on the card instead. To use the word in Spanish. Doing this on your phone is very simple, install a free flashcard app like Quizlet or AnkiApp and upload your photos.

Instead Of Lists

Choose words that are important to your everyday activities and how you communicate with others.

This is one way of acquiring vocabulary for a new career. Rather than reciting endless work lists, begin with your own, your partner's, parents, or friends. You'll have a greater chance of recalling it if you use it regularly.

Keep a diary of your feelings.

Using new words to discuss your own life and experiences, describing your feelings, concepts, and past experience what you see in textbooks is just the beginning of your schooling. This is using real-life words in a natural and meaningful manner.

3. Repeat effectively

Some people can easily remember entire tables of verbs in English or French that they learned in school; however, ask these people to conjugate them, use them in context or use them to tell a story... and then understand why repeating for the sake of repeating is not always the best option.

Learning by repetition has certain benefits; the secret is to do it effectively.

Spaced repetition is better for studying because you just need to concentrate on one thing at a time.

Gabriel Wyner outlines his spaced repetition learning technique in his book Fluent Forever: How to Understand Every Language and Never Lose It. Instead of spending an hour memorizing all at once, consider repeatedly learning new words over increasingly long periods.

Goals like making the brain retain new vocabulary right as it forgets. As Wyner notes, "To learn and keep 3,600 flashcards, you can spend 30 minutes every day for four months.

Be more visual

Remember what we mentioned about personalizing your learning by using your photos on your flashcards?

Doing this will not only help your brain memorize better; you can also use images from Google Images to use on your flashcards to help you memorize. Try to give your cards a fun touch; use images of places that are familiar to you, vacation photos, or the faces of your acquaintances. It will be much easier to remember than to just use words.

Repeat and put into practice what you learned immediately

Learning verb lists is not the same as knowing how to use them; it is easier for our brain to remember words when we use them in everyday conversation.

Putting into practice what you learned by talking with your teacher, classmates or groups is crucial; in this way, you will motivate yourself to continue learning. You can also practice writing ten different sentences using the word you learned; repeating the word with a context will help you remember it and help you understand it.

How do you learn several languages simultaneously?

"Will you study several languages at the same time, and if so, how do I go about doing it?" It is also possible to learn more than one language at the same time. I want to first articulate my feelings on this before sending out some advice.

I only taught one language at a time. As I remember, my monolingual approach was directed specifically at three reasons: (1) I was never in a hurry to learn other languages, (2) once I had picked a language, I was thoroughly immersed in the learning process, and (3) I benefited from having only one language to work on at a time. Next, I will expand on these considerations.

Language acquisition is negatively influenced by the industrial world's here and now' urge. It should not be shocking that there is a long list of Italian proverbs warning us of the negative implications of rushing. Haste is a poor advisor, slow and steady wins the race, and so on. Learning takes place over the first six months, and a great deal of focus and commitment are expected during this period. If time is split among two, three, or even four separate tasks, the quality of your learning will suffer. Hence Google's automatic translation

Building a base

Words, structures, and sounds are used throughout the language learning process, but they are often accompanied by thoughts, colors, pictures, and memories. If you wish to keep your language alive in your brain, you must learn this central language. Additionally, it takes time to construct a language core, which results in overlapping or stopping languages from being learned properly.

Optimizing your time

Doing a foreign language does not deter you from improving or retaining what you already know at a higher level. The secret is time management skills. You'd like to find sustainable language learning programming through trial and error.

Two Students Race

I use the word 'term of a boss' to represent what I mean by 'the race of the two students.' Two students, both Italian, enter a challenge to master ten languages. The judges give them a "time budget," ten years. A student chooses to learn two languages every two years. Next, learn English and Spanish. Pick up French and German after two years. Although learning French and German, he loves interacting with fluent native speakers in both English and Spanish. He likes to read, too. After the fourth year, he will speak German and French well enough to continue studying Portuguese and Swedish. When you go to Paris, you will use your knowledge of four languages to boost your proficiency in Portuguese and Swedish. On the six-year point, he chooses to study Mandarin and Romanian. Two years later, he reads Japanese and Dutch. Ten years back, after the time limit is up, he is fluent in English, Spanish, French, English, Portuguese, Swedish, Mandarin Chinese, and Romanian. Has few languages; however, it provided a center of more than five languages. Even you will never lose these five languages. He will rust on them, but they will return to him.

Student B takes the same language routes but prefers a learning approach that begins for all ten languages at once. He has traditionally lacked continuity and patience when trying to learn additional languages. Some days he knows five, six, or seven times, but not all ten. However, languages were taken to a simple level by this case. Languages include Italian, Spanish, Dutch, and German. This is because the student neglected to construct a linguistic core with either language.

Let's use an extreme case, but it shows the general idea. Multitasking tricks people into assuming that it helps to learn, when in fact, it destroys the learning process. It's like the tortoise, including the hare, right? Become the turtle. Patience will help you excel.

Multiple Language Acquisition Tips and Advice

I learned a new language every two years and studied developing my current ones over the past 20 years. My method for learning a foreign language takes about two years. At the same time, if you intend to pick up more than one phrase, be sure to include the following:

- Enough Time To Devote To Language Learning
- Self-Control
- Experience In Language Acquisition
- Flexible Time Scheduling
- Edicon-2112 profile photo

Here are few tips to help you with your multilingual challenge.

Choose a choice of two languages Three languages will damage any language core you are attempting to create.

Select two languages that are separate from each other. Possibly overlaps are created by phrases, syntax, feelings, and so on, resulting in uncertainty. Therefore, mastering two languages at the same time is not a smart idea.

Choose a "simple" language and a very "difficult" one (I explain this concept in both English and Spanish on YouTube)

Select two languages, offering the difficult language 70-80% of your time and the "free" language 20-30% of your time.

Study both languages daily.

Edicon2112 Avatar

Slow down. Learning a foreign language takes time, quality work, and persistence. A language is an adventure. No hard and quick rules exist for learning one thing at a time. Know the situations you will face while embarking on several journeys. Consider the five suggestions given above.

Don't you plan to learn a foreign language in school?

Are you fluent in a language but can't speak it? Is language grammar still a priority for you? Or can you work on language learning and at a quick pace? Is A + B still equivalent to C for you? If you agree with one of these questions, expect to be shocked! The easiest way to understand a language is to talk or think about it. This article incorporates certain facts and insights that will revolutionize your mindset.

They tell us about Barney and Sally at kindergarten and what they like to read, watch, or put in their sandwiches. As for if Barney wants tomatoes on his burgers, or if Sally called her parents, I couldn't care less. A language is not only about hearing about an imaginary character being interested in childhood events, but rather a path that leads to a deep academic transition. Many textbooks discuss various versions and variants of Barney and Sally and their families. Cold grammar and unpleasant words are learned alongside each other.

One second, if I can. What motivates you to know a foreign language? Consider this: Pause for a minute to actually care about what you're reading. Why did you start learning another language? Do you want to master tens of thousands of new and unusual words? You're waiting for something that can enlighten you, aren't you? My best bet is that all of you said "No!" Excellent. We are in for something big.

For a moment, let's explore your mother tongue. When you speak your native language, do you not care about the vocabulary you are using and the tenses you are adding to verbs?" As a consequence, you don't need any syntax or sentence construction assistance. I guess it is a little ridiculous to say, but the idea is to familiarize yourself with your target language so that you never need assistance with it. "Oh, Mladen, but how do you do this?" It's easy. The next paragraph includes guidance on how to develop your spoken language skills.

Right now, I have talked about all the normal language learning errors and people in general. Now is the time for "How."

Clear your mind such that you can properly understand the language you are learning. Imagine stuff that you haven't even imagined.

Don't be afraid to make mistakes! Using a friend from your neighborhood or sign up for Skype to learn a language with whom you can speak at least 2 to 3 days per week. You may make several mistakes at the outset, and you will feel ashamed. Don't talk about it! It is the anticipated result.

Don't believe people would view you negatively if you make mistakes! - People want to show you their words. Particularly at the polyglot club. They aren't kidding because you don't know the vocabulary yet.

Don't be timid! There is no embarrassment in telling anyone about their lives. Some of the better subjects are: What did you do during the day? What are your plans for tomorrow?

Introduce yourself! Concentrate on yesterday, "what ifs," and future holidays. Establishing new friendships.

Blog about your days! Ask your new friend if they wouldn't mind repairing any mistakes that you've made. Identify mistakes you've made.

Will Neurophysiology Help You Understand A Language?

Awareness of human language may almost be a necessary trait to qualify us as "Homo sapiens."

In reality, fluency in a language is dependent in part on genetics.

Additionally, genetic mutations can affect many facets of language acquisition, such as aphasia and apraxia (FOXp2, microdeletion 22q11, addition or deletion of an X or Y chromosome).

Genetic inheritance has a non-negligible effect on language acquisition.

Our voice also expresses our climate.

Adaptation of our neuronal circuit and neural cells to the world converts the information we gain every day.

Our entire civilization will be transferred to our descendants by way of this circuit.

This is an outstanding example of an infant mastering a language while living with a native speaker without studying.

Genetics and the climate of language-learning go hand in hand.

In reality, a lack of adjustment to our neural relation and the regulation of our gene expression inhibits our ability to interpret the world and to learn a new language.

Acquisition Of Vocabulary

All should learn a foreign language. Using this skill effectively requires paying attention to LAD (language learning device). International grammar constitutes the bare bones of all languages.

Your unborn baby just needs to cover this 'skeleton' with a 'suitable skin' over it. It is difficult for an instinct-deprived infant to build a skeleton. Instinctually learning a language is not straightforward.

As an analogy, think of a haystack with 100 needles in it. In 100 hours, 100 people can find 50-60 needles using their eyes and hands. Kids will locate all the needles in 10 minutes. No one suggests that the boy did an outstanding job using only his eyes and hands. The infant is believed to be using a magnet or other "kit."

Once we meet with a variety of linguists, we can learn that they use general problem-solving methods to solve just a fraction of the grammar puzzle. A 5-6-year-old kid will not be able to solve all the "puzzles." At this point, we can easily see that we must gain information, not just practice it.

In the end, the opportunity to learn a foreign language is important. Struggling with grammar isn't important to learn a foreign language. People skills are of primary significance.

Plainly, we learn our vocabulary as children, not as adults. You should concentrate on simple items to avoid complex verb tenses or rules.

Steps To Earn Money Online...
Speaking In Spanish!

You don't know yet, but when you finish reading this article, you will be totally surprised.

Why?

Because right now, you have such an obvious ability, but SO obvious, that you probably haven't realized you have it.

You can earn money doing translations, from any country in the world and from the comfort of your home, just as I have been doing for a long time:

But there is also another activity that you can do that can help you even more to make a profit.

How?

Simple: Speaking in Spanish with other people!

But how is this possible?

It works like this:

Around the world, there are hundreds, thousands, and THOUSANDS of people who are NOT Spanish-speakers but who are interested in learning and practicing their Spanish.

Much of them are from countries such as United States, England, Canada, Australia, France, Germany, and many others.

However, many of them, instead of going to formal classes in a language institute or academy, prefer to use the facilities and flexibility that the Internet offers us today.

It is easier to talk to someone who already speaks Spanish and is their native language on a flexible schedule, including at a lower cost, rather than attending a language institute in England, for example, dealing with traffic, rigid class schedules, and a high price.

On the other hand, many prefer to learn to speak the "real" Spanish, which people speak in everyday life, rather than the Spanish that is learned from books within the four walls of a classroom.

And this is where you can come in to help them, in exchange for generous payments.

Here are steps you have to follow to start making money speaking Spanish:

Step 1:

Identify WHERE are the people who are looking for you so that they can speak in Spanish with you. You don't have to look everywhere… since not everyone wants to learn to speak our language. However, there are very specific places where they are. This is where you have to look for them.

Step 2:

Show them that you are one of the right people to help them. For this, you have to know WHAT to say and HOW to say it, so that they accept you and can give you their money in exchange for talking to you in Spanish.

Step 3:

Implement a system of "packages" that allows you to access more and more people who want to speak in Spanish with you. In such a way that when you want to earn some more extra money, you simply speak in Spanish… and voila!

The truth is that there are tools like SKYPE that make the process much easier. There are also different means of payment that help to collect the profits that are obtained, even if you are in any Latin country or anywhere in the world.

It is worth mentioning that if you decide to join our program, you will additionally receive as a gift access to the "Earn Money Speaking In Spanish" area, where all the details that have been mentioned in the previous three steps are delved into so that you can start sooner.

Give Spanish Classes Online, Earn Money Teaching

To teach Spanish, you will first have to learn the necessary techniques to do so, but don't worry, because you have 3-4 week courses that you can do online, some even specifically designed to teach Spanish online, such as the following ELE course International:

Course to teach Spanish online

Once you have the necessary knowledge, you can work as a Spanish teacher from anywhere in the world, thanks to online teaching platforms that facilitate virtual and live classes with native teachers.

Earn money giving Spanish classes online!

Preply

Online teacher platform, in this case of any subject, but above all focused on language teaching.

You can register as a Spanish teacher, so that anyone in the world who wants to teach with you can contact you and thus hire you.

In addition, they have a section with classified ads of people looking for Spanish teachers. Each one puts the type of teacher they need and how much they can pay, so that, if you are interested, you can get in touch and make your offer.

Ads from people looking for Spanish teachers

It is advisable to begin with a low rate , in order to win students who leave you good comments and build your own personal brand and be considered a great teacher.

Amazing talker

Very Preply style and with a very simple and attractive design.

It has a simulator with which it tells you the money you can earn based on the hours you work and the language you teach and according to which you could earn around € 1,800 teaching Spanish 40 hours a week.

Iboux

In this online language teaching platform they only accept native and certified teachers. If they choose you, they guarantee you a number of hours per week and they have a team and a program to facilitate the classes they give you.

Tandem

This is a language exchange app used by millions of people, with which you can get in touch with other users to speak and practice languages.

It is very easy to use, each user puts his mother tongue, the languages he speaks and the ones he is interested in practicing.

In addition, it has a section in which you can register as a tutor so that users who want to can hire Spanish classes for 20, 40, 60 or 90 minutes.

According to their page, you can earn up to $ 500 a month for teaching a couple of hours a day. You need to have a certified ELE Teacher qualification in order to apply as a language teacher.

SuperProof

This is another of the main platforms to offer and receive private classes of any type of subject and among them, of course, is Spanish as one of the most demanded.

The good thing about this platform is that anyone can join, you don't even need to have a degree that certifies your training, but it is clear that the more prepared you are, the better you will do.

Lingoda

Another platform for online language courses with native teachers, including the teaching of Spanish.

You have to send your application to be accepted and if you pass the tests, you will be able to work for them and start earning money for your Spanish classes, with the students that they are getting you. You choose the hours you want to work.

You have to know how to speak English and have a degree or certificate to teach Spanish.

Italki

In Italki you can also learn any language you want and of course, earn money teaching the ones you know. Here, not everyone can register; you have to wait for vacancies in your language. This is fine, because having greater control, once you are inside you will not have to fight with as much competition as you can with other platforms in which everyone can sign up.

It gives options to work teaching languages both to native professionals with experience or accredited training and to others who do it in a more informal way.

Glassgap

This platform is created in Spain and you can not only give Spanish classes online and charge for it , but also for any other subject in which you are a specialist. You put your prices and they put the virtual classroom you need to teach.

Verbling

Online teaching platform only for language teachers.

You just have to set your rates, set your schedule and wait to receive interested students in your classes.

Footprints Recruitment

This agency decides to recruit teachers to work in foreign countries and also does it to work remotely. As stated on the page you can earn up to $ 22 an hour working with them. They are oriented to the Asian market and although most of the teachers they need are to teach English, they also need Spanish teachers on some occasions.

Now, you already know how to earn money giving Spanish classes online!

More Sites To TEACH SPANISH Online (Up To $ 30 USD Per Hour) + Companies That Are HIRING

Generally, you will get better returns by teaching Spanish on your own. This is because you will be building a passive income that continues to work for you, even while dedicating your time to other activities. Some of the methods we will share below can generate anywhere from $ 1,000 to $ 3,500 per month (although, like any business, it will take some time to reach that level of profit).

By working teaching Spanish for a company, you can earn between $ 10 to $ 30 per hour, depending on the company and your level of experience. In the list below, you can find the companies that are hiring at the moment and details about the application process.

What do you need to earn money teaching Spanish?

There are no special requirements to earn money teaching Spanish on your own. Although it is recommended to have a university degree in languages, the reality is that there are many people obtaining constant income without any type of university training.

Requirements to start earning money teaching Spanish online:

Being over 18 years

Speak Spanish fluently (diction and spelling at native level)

Decent webcam, to record yourself training others by video conference (we recommend this camera)

Powerful microphone with good audio quality (we recommend this inexpensive microphone)

Computer / Basic Computer

Reliable internet connection

Requirements to teach Spanish online may include a high school or college degree, previous teaching experience, a TEFL certificate, or perhaps an online interview.

Although the companies that will hire you to work teaching Spanish online have different requirements, generally, it isn't crucial to have a license for these jobs.

However, having a language teaching license (known as the TEFL, ELE, or QTS certification) will help you earn a better salary when working with these companies.

How to earn money teaching Spanish online (on your own)

In 2021, there is good earning potential to make money teaching Spanish online. This industry is not that competitive these days, so there is a good opportunity to generate income.

Here are some ways to earn money teaching our language to good effect this year:

1. Your own educational blog

Starting your own blog is one of our recommended ways to earn money from home in 2021. Creating a blog is much easier than it sounds (we show you how to do it in less than 30 minutes), and it has never been so cheap to maintain your own blog (it will only cost you $ 2.25 per month).

We recommend WordPress to start your own blog. These are the steps to follow:

- Sign up with a fast hosting and free domain (we recommend Hostgator)
- Create your blog using WordPress
- Choose a theme or a template for your site.
- Start posting Spanish lessons.

How will you earn money then? The ways to make money from a blog are limitless! But the easiest way to start making money is through banner ads (we recommend Google AdSense).

Always make sure to add posts to your blog regularly and start getting subscribers to your email list.

After spending some time with your blog, you will be able to combine it with more forms of money by teaching Spanish. For example, you could:

- Sell Spanish course packages and other educational products.
- Make money from affiliate links (who pay you a commission for related products, like books) while blogging.
- Combine your blog lessons with your own YouTube channel

Much more!

2. Create your own Spanish course

Creating a course is a great way to earn money teaching Spanish online. Best of all: you will be creating a PASSIVE INCOME. You have to do the job once, and you can keep earning for a long time.

You can start getting money with this method by creating a complete Spanish course and selling it in sections or as a complete unit.

For the best returns, we recommend tailoring your course to a key audience. For example, create a course teaching Spanish to teenagers.

Before offering your course, spend some time evaluating the competition and work on improving something that is missing. This way, you can create a simpler learning process and have better earnings.

We recommend uploading your Spanish course to the Udemy learning platform, which will help you sell it with little effort.

3. Books teaching Spanish with Amazon

One of our FAVORITE ways to make money online in 2021 is Kindle e-books. You will be amazed at the growth and profit you can make with this method.

Amazon Kindle books are a great way to teach Spanish online.

Getting started is extremely easy. Amazon will allow you to publish your own book and sell it around the world for a low price (usually between $ 0.99 to $ 2.99).

Although the price of the book is usually low, the secret to earning constant income is to publish more than one book. That is, you can teach Spanish by dividing your course into several volumes that your audience can buy for one low price.

For example, you can divide your course into different books or modules (such as basic, intermediate, and advanced.) You can passively earn thousands of dollars a month with this method.

In addition, by uploading your book to the Kindle publishing platform, you will become a published author, which will give you greater credibility as someone who teaches Spanish, and you can establish yourself as an authority in the industry.

4. YouTube channel to teach Spanish

In 2021, YouTube is fast becoming the # 1 place to teach and make money online. A Spanish course fits this reality perfectly.

There are simple videos (for example, how to pronounce the word beggar) that have thousands of views. By becoming a YouTube partner or partner, you can passively earn money for every view your video receives.

Best of all: There is clearly a great demand for Spanish teaching videos. Take, for example, this trend in Google searches.

To earn money teaching Spanish on YouTube, you will need:

- A decent camera for recording (we recommend this model)
- A cheap microphone (we use this one)
- A computer capable of editing videos with a reliable internet connection

NOTE: Although you can use your cell phone to record, it is not recommended since the video and audio quality will not be the same.

YouTube accounts are free, so this method is perfect for making money online without investing.

After posting some videos teaching Spanish, you will start to get more followers and watch your earnings climb. You can also partner with the best affiliate programs of 2021 to generate a good amount of income.

Also, if you become a reliable channel to learn Spanish, you may earn money promoting products on your channel.

Earn money by teaching Spanish WORKING for a company

Several companies are hiring and offering you jobs teaching live Spanish classes. You will be paid to be an online tutor and help others improve Spanish pronunciation.

Best of all, this is a job that allows you to earn money from anywhere in the world.

With a strong connection and a decent webcam, you can work teaching Spanish online, no matter where you are.

Most of these companies allow you to work your own hours and earn IN DOLLARS, but that's not the best part...

You can also set your own rates. Although you will need to accumulate some experience (as with any job), most of these sites allow you to set your own rates by building a good reputation with them.

You will be able to set your higher rates by accumulating good comments on your profile and thus earn even more money teaching Spanish online.

These are the unique companies to work for teaching Spanish online:

1. Verbling

Hourly wage: from $ 7 to $ 30 (USD)

Verbling is an online website where language learners can take classes with tutors. This company hires people from all over the world to teach languages (including Spanish) to students and business entrepreneurs.

To apply for these jobs, the human resources staff reviews all applications from prospective tutors. Although the application process takes some time, after being accepted, you can start to earn money teaching Spanish online.

The job consists of giving lessons through videoconferencing, so you will be interacting with students from various parts of the world.

Students are generally very satisfied with the tutoring services. The company claims that more than 70% of its users recommend the company to their friends.

2. iTalki

Hourly wage: $ 10 to $ 30 dollars (USD)

iTalki's mission is to facilitate fluency when learning any foreign language. This company is hiring staff to help others improve their Spanish and other language skills (such as English, Mandarin, German, and more)

It has a global community of more than one million students and more than ten languages. Every day, more students and teachers discover how fast they can learn with personal online lessons.

3. Verbal Planet

Hourly rate: $ 10 to $ 30 dollars

VerbalPlanet is a reputable language teaching service that facilitates online Spanish classes (as well as other languages).

The company is looking for native language tutors around the world willing to teach Spanish online using the Skype service.

They have an innovative approach to learning a foreign language, and the compensation is one of the largest in the industry.

4. Lingoda

Hourly wage: Varies based on your experience

Lingoda is a very innovative website that offers group sessions for people who are learning languages, including Spanish.

They are hiring Spanish tutors willing to make language learning easier and more accessible. Their mission is to reduce the time and discomfort of going to a language school and improve pronunciation by employing native speakers.

Best of all: They don't require any experience, so it's a good place to start if you don't have any.

5. Cambly

Hourly wage varies. They pay you by the minute.

Cambly is a tutoring website dedicated to people who want to learn English but with expansion plans for the Spanish language. Unlike most others, you are paid by the minute, not by the hour.

To work with this company, you must meet these requirements:

- Be a native Spanish speaker.
- Have earned a degree or be enrolled in a college program
- Prefer those with previous experience teaching children
- Outgoing personality
- Available to teach at least 6 hours (12 classes) per week
- You can see all the details in the Cambly jobs section.

Earning money taught Spanish online:

- There is no better time to earn money teaching Spanish. Thanks to the Internet, it is possible to build a 100% passive source of income or to work from anywhere teaching our language to others.
- Whether you choose to start a YouTube channel to teach Spanish or work for a

company, the truth is that teaching Spanish to others offers a good amount of profit.

If you have more questions about how to make money teaching Spanish online or companies that are hiring Spanish tutors, leave us a comment, and we will do our best to help you.

Summary and Conclusion

Spanish and its importance in the world

The Spanish, the language of the future

The Spanish language is important in the world, they have tried to displace it by others, but due to the efforts of the language-speaking countries, it has been possible to keep it in force, since due to its great extension it is difficult to change some customs already established and rooted in a society.

Spanish will set the standard in a few years, forming a fundamental part for academies, for business and other aspects in which our language can be present.

General features

To begin, it is important to highlight the meaning of the word language understood as a language, a human representation and a form of verbal or written communication typical of a community.

Spanish is also known as Castilian by reference to Castile, where it was spoken before its expansion to Hispanic descent from Vulgar Latin.

Through language, people's feelings and thoughts can be made known through oral or written expression, which appears thanks to language and the search for human interaction.

Spanish is the second most widely spoken language and one of the most difficult to learn in the world, as it presents a very extensive meaning in its words, lending itself to the interpretation of a term in various senses, which we know as polysemy.

In each Hispanic country there are words of their own culture, which are not shared with other nations and communities, where a uniform language is not presented and due to its complexity it does not allow the understanding of some people with others due to their differences.

Transformation of Spanish

The language has acquired loanwords from other languages, which vary according to the country of the speaker, where individuals displace terms from their own culture, adopting the new, the strange.

In Spanish-speaking countries there are still archaisms that are used mainly by people who live in the countryside and who are of an adult age.

The way of speaking and expressing oneself before others depends on the culture and in this way creates an image, since the language of a person from the street is not the same as that of a person with some type of academic preparation, since the management of vocabulary gives a social status that is recognized at first glance.

Spanish is a changing sphere that creates new words, which can become degradation or scandal for the time of grandparents and ancestors, as is the case of what is known as parlache, which is the language of people who speak a lot without contribute nothing.

Every culture has its customs, customs that vary over the years, that is the example of Spanish, because it is implemented in society as a form of expression, which is subject to change by presenting new proposals, which are studied and accepted or not by the Royal Academy of the Spanish Language.

Diffusion of Spanish

In European countries and America where their language is not Spanish, they are implementing the teaching of this language as a foreign language, since there are more than 400 million speakers in the world, as it is a unified language seeking that people from different countries and regions can be easily understood.

In Africa, both Spanish and French are considered diplomatic languages used at specific events.

INDIGENOUS PEOPLE PROMOTE THEIR DIALECT

In Spanish-speaking countries, it is also worth mentioning the indigenous communities that have their own dialect, but because man is a curious being and seeks rapprochement with others, he creates and carries out new strategies to have access and ease of going beyond the own vocabulary, because you are in a society where there is a recognition of the strange, thus achieving a greater understanding between people of other cultures, regions and countries.

It is worth recognizing the work that indigenous people have done over the years, a work of patriotism or a sense of belonging, since each time they seek to fight for their rights and prevent them from changing their customs and dialect; They are united communities that are in search of recognition within society, as people rooted in roots that do not want to change, of which they feel proud and do not allow themselves to be offended when a stranger enters with the intention of transforming some aspect.

The globalization has consequences for the Spanish

Spanish is increasingly changing due to many factors, including the globalization of markets and the entry of foreign investors to each of the Spanish-speaking countries, bringing with it the so-called foreigners that are used more day by day and are included in our lexicon.

It is evident that the market and large industries try to homogenize people's tastes, needs and customs through exports and imports from where they are acquired and using terms from other places.

Our language opens up a wide range of possibilities for us; Taking Latin America as an example, with the support of some countries with others, it has undergone changes and evolutions against the great powers in the world, although it does not generate great competitiveness, it has shown that despite its economic difficulties it can make progress and be fundamental part for the other states of the world.

At present, a tangible example is the initiation and closing of treaties of free trade, which the Andean countries to reach an agreement and seek to improve economic relations between their countries, obtained somehow because the Spanish in these cases is the fundamental basis for achieving an understanding.

Deterioration of the tongue

Studies made by the members of the Royal Academy of the Language highlight the misuse of some words of our language, leading them to include these terms in the texts, since the common becomes custom and sometimes it is difficult to erase from societies where they are already have implemented.

The deterioration of Spanish is increasingly notorious, as we invent and adopt new ways of speaking that are not recognized and legal for specialists on the subject, but are typical of groups that belong to a society.

One hundred years of loneliness

According to Tomás Eloy Martínez, Argentine journalist and writer affirms that " One Hundred Years of Solitude opened for our Spanish the doors of imagination", is a book that gave and is still going around the world, and that it is part of the recognition of the work that Gabriel García Márquez has carried out as a great writer.

Creator of Macondo, an expert in mixing reality with fantasy, famous for his Nobel Prize in literature and today for its 80 years of existence; The IV Congress of the Spanish Language that took place in Cartagena began with a tribute to his work and dedication at the time of writing and in some way to give life to our language, Spanish with his literary works.